Mastering Arduino

Hands-On Projects for Beginners and Experts Build and program innovative electronic projects with Arduino

THOMPSON CARTER

Table of Content

TABLE OF CONTENTS

Introduction

Mastering Arduino: Hands-On Projects for Beginners and Experts

In the world of electronics and embedded systems, Arduino has become a household name. Whether you're a beginner or an expert, Arduino offers an open-source platform that makes it possible to bring ideas to life. From simple DIY projects to complex, innovative solutions, Arduino has proven to be the go-to tool for makers, hobbyists, engineers, and educators around the globe. This book, **Mastering Arduino: Hands-On Projects for Beginners and Experts**, is your comprehensive guide to understanding and harnessing the power of Arduino to create real-world applications.

Why Arduino?

Arduino has transformed the way we interact with electronics. It combines hardware and software in an accessible, user-friendly environment that allows people of all skill levels to start building their own interactive projects quickly and efficiently. Whether you're interested in

automating your home, designing **wearable technology**, or developing **robotic systems**, Arduino provides the foundation for creating virtually any embedded system you can imagine.

What Will You Learn in This Book?

This book is designed for anyone who wants to dive into the world of Arduino, whether you are a beginner who has never worked with electronics or an experienced maker looking to expand your skills. It will take you step-by-step through the process of building your own Arduino-based systems, starting from the basics and advancing to more complex projects.

Target Audience

- **Beginners**: If you're new to Arduino or electronics, this book will walk you through everything you need to know to get started. From installing the Arduino IDE to connecting basic sensors, you will learn by doing through practical, hands-on examples.
- **Intermediate and Advanced Users**: For those with some experience in electronics or programming, this book will push your skills further. It covers complex

topics like **IoT (Internet of Things)** projects, **power management, PCB design**, and more. You'll tackle more sophisticated projects and explore ways to integrate Arduino with other platforms, including cloud services and wireless communication.

- **Educators and Makers**: This book can also be used as a learning tool for teaching others about electronics. With clear explanations, code examples, and a variety of project-based learning opportunities, educators can use this as a curriculum for teaching Arduino.

What Makes This Book Different?

Unlike many technical books that focus solely on theory or specific types of projects, this book provides a **balanced approach** by combining solid theory with practical, real-world projects. You will not only learn the **basics of Arduino programming**, but you'll also gain in-depth experience with a range of components and sensors. Each chapter is designed to challenge you with increasingly complex projects that will build upon what you learned in previous chapters.

Here's what makes this book stand out:

1. **Comprehensive Coverage**: It spans all levels, from absolute beginners to advanced users. Whether you're interested in building a simple **LED blink circuit** or developing a **smart home automation system**, this book has you covered.

2. **Hands-on Projects**: Every chapter includes hands-on projects that give you the opportunity to build something real. These projects are designed to reinforce the concepts you've learned while encouraging creativity and experimentation.

3. **Clear, Easy-to-Understand Writing**: Arduino projects can sometimes be overwhelming, but this book breaks down complex topics into bite-sized pieces, using clear explanations and diagrams to guide you through the process.

4. **Diverse Applications**: The book covers a wide range of applications—from basic sensor reading to building **IoT-based systems**, **robotics**, **wearable technology**, and **home automation systems**.

What You Will Build

Through this book, you will embark on a journey where you will create a variety of projects that illustrate the power and versatility of Arduino:

- **Basic Projects**: You'll start by building simple circuits, like a **temperature sensor**, a **motion detector**, and a **LED control system**.

- **Advanced Projects**: As you gain confidence, you'll build projects like an **environmental monitoring system**, a **step counter for fitness tracking**, and a **smart home automation system**.

- **Interfacing with Other Platforms**: You'll also learn how to integrate Arduino with platforms like **Raspberry Pi**, **Google Firebase**, and **cloud services**, enabling remote monitoring and control of your projects.

- **Custom Hardware Design**: You'll even design your own **custom shields** and **PCBs** to create tailored solutions for your projects.

How This Book Is Structured

This book is broken down into **27 chapters**, each focusing on a specific aspect of working with Arduino. Here's a brief overview of the chapters:

1. **Getting Started with Arduino**: Setting up your first Arduino environment and basic projects.

2. **The Arduino Programming Language**: Diving into the core of Arduino programming with variables, functions, and loops.

3. **Working with Sensors and Actuators**: Interfacing sensors like temperature, motion, and light sensors to control real-world devices.

4. **Wireless Communication**: Integrating wireless communication technologies like Bluetooth and Wi-Fi.

5. **Arduino for IoT**: Learning how to connect Arduino to the cloud and build IoT applications.

6. **Low-Power and Battery-Powered Projects**: Power management strategies to optimize battery life for portable systems.

7. **Building Wearable Technology**: Using Arduino to build fitness trackers, smartwatches, and other wearables.

8. **Designing Custom PCBs and Shields**: Learning how to design and fabricate your own custom hardware to expand your Arduino projects.

9. **Advanced Arduino Projects**: Creating sophisticated systems, from environmental monitoring to robotics and home automation.

Conclusion

Whether you're building a **smart home system**, a **robot**, or a **fitness tracker**, this book will provide you with the tools and knowledge you need to turn your ideas into reality. By the end of the book, you will have mastered Arduino programming, learned how to integrate various sensors and actuators, and explored a wide range of applications, from IoT and wearable tech to custom hardware design.

This book is more than just a guide to Arduino; it's a hands-on learning experience that will teach you how to build real-world solutions and inspire you to innovate. Arduino is a powerful platform, and with the skills you'll gain here, the possibilities are endless. So, let's get started on this exciting journey to master Arduino and bring your projects to life!

CHAPTER 1

INTRODUCTION TO ARDUINO

In this chapter, we will lay the groundwork for your Arduino journey by introducing you to its core concepts, its evolution, and why it has become such a versatile and powerful tool in the world of electronics. By the end of this chapter, you'll have a solid understanding of what Arduino is, its potential, and the essential components you'll work with in upcoming projects.

Understanding Arduino and Its Potential

Arduino is an open-source electronics platform based on simple software and hardware. It consists of a microcontroller (the brain of your project), a development environment to write and upload programs, and an easy-to-use interface for communication with sensors, motors, lights, and more. The beauty of Arduino is its versatility—it can be used to build anything from simple light-control systems to complex robotics and automation systems.

What makes Arduino stand out is its accessibility to beginners while still providing powerful capabilities for advanced users. It allows you to dive right into hands-on experimentation, allowing your creativity to shape innovative projects without needing deep knowledge in complex electronics.

History and Evolution of Arduino

Arduino was created in 2005 by a group of Italian designers and engineers, led by Massimo Banzi and David Cuartielles, who wanted to create a more affordable and flexible way for students and designers to prototype electronic projects. It was initially designed for interactive projects in the field of design and art but quickly gained popularity in the broader electronics community.

Over the years, Arduino's ecosystem has expanded exponentially. Today, there are many variations of the Arduino board to cater to specific needs, such as the Arduino Uno (the most common board), the Arduino Mega (for projects requiring more I/O pins), and the Arduino Nano (compact for small projects). Arduino boards have evolved to incorporate new features, higher performance, and improved compatibility with other technology, making it a great choice for anything from educational projects to cutting-edge innovations.

What Makes Arduino a Powerful Tool for Electronic Projects

Arduino's strength lies in its simplicity and flexibility. Here's what makes it such an essential tool in the electronics and DIY community:

- **Open-source platform**: Both hardware and software are open-source, meaning anyone can modify and improve them. This allows for constant innovation and a large community of developers and enthusiasts to share their knowledge and ideas.
- **Wide community support**: Arduino has one of the most active and supportive online communities. Whether you're a beginner or an expert, you'll find countless tutorials, forums, and project guides to help you.
- **Ease of use**: The Arduino IDE (Integrated Development Environment) is intuitive, making it easy to write and upload code to the Arduino board. The programming language is based on C/C++ but simplified for ease of learning.

- **Flexibility**: You can connect Arduino to a wide range of sensors, actuators, displays, and other electronic components. This flexibility allows you to work on almost any kind of project—from automation systems and robotics to data logging and weather stations.

- **Low-cost hardware**: Arduino boards are inexpensive, making them an excellent choice for hobbyists, educators, and those who want to prototype quickly without high costs.

These attributes combine to make Arduino a powerful tool for turning ideas into reality, whether you're just starting out in electronics or building sophisticated devices.

Overview of Common Components Used with Arduino

To create functional Arduino projects, you'll need to understand some of the common components that work alongside your Arduino board. Here's a quick overview of the essential components you'll encounter:

- **LEDs**: Light-emitting diodes are one of the simplest components. They're often used to indicate the status of your project or to create visual effects.

- **Resistors**: Resistors are used to limit the current flowing through components like LEDs. Understanding how to use them correctly is crucial for safe and efficient circuit design.

- **Sensors**: Sensors detect physical properties like light, temperature, humidity, or motion. Common sensors include:

  o **Temperature sensor (e.g., LM35)** for reading temperature.

  o **Light sensor (e.g., LDR)** for detecting light levels.

  o **Motion sensors (e.g., PIR)** for detecting movement.

- **Motors**: Motors are used to produce motion. You'll work with various types such as DC motors, stepper motors, and servos.

- **Displays**: Displays such as 7-segment LED displays and LCD screens are used to show output data like numbers or text.

- **Breadboards and Wires**: A breadboard is an essential tool for prototyping your projects, while wires connect all your components to the Arduino board.

- **Power Supply**: Depending on your project, you may need a power supply to ensure your Arduino and components get the required voltage.

These components will form the building blocks for the various projects in this book, and you'll get hands-on experience with them in upcoming chapters. As you progress, you'll also learn about advanced components, like wireless communication modules (Bluetooth, Wi-Fi) and even advanced sensors for complex systems.

By the end of this chapter, you should have a solid grasp of what Arduino is, its history, why it's such a powerful tool, and the key components you'll need to start building your own projects. Ready to move on to the next step? Let's start exploring the hardware and software environment in the next chapter!

CHAPTER 2

GETTING STARTED WITH ARDUINO

Now that you have an understanding of Arduino and its potential, it's time to get your hands dirty with some real-world applications. This chapter will guide you through the process of setting up everything you need to start building projects using Arduino, from choosing the right board to installing the development environment and running your first simple project.

How to Choose the Right Arduino Board for Your Project

Choosing the right Arduino board is crucial for the success of your project. There are several boards available, each suited for different types of projects. Here's a quick overview of some of the most common Arduino boards and how to choose the right one for your needs:

- **Arduino Uno**: This is the most popular and versatile board for beginners. It's ideal for most basic projects, such as controlling LEDs, sensors, and motors. If you're just starting out, this board is a great choice.

- **Arduino Mega**: If your project requires more I/O pins (such as in larger, more complex systems or projects with a lot of sensors and actuators), the Arduino Mega is a better choice. It offers more pins and memory compared to the Uno.

- **Arduino Nano**: A smaller version of the Uno, the Nano is perfect for projects that need a compact design, such as wearables or space-limited projects. Despite its smaller size, it has similar capabilities to the Uno.

- **Arduino Leonardo**: This board has a unique feature: it can emulate a keyboard or mouse, making it great for projects that need human interface devices (HID) capabilities.

- **Arduino Due**: If your project requires more processing power or if you're working with more complex algorithms or signals, the Arduino Due offers a 32-bit ARM core, providing a significant performance boost.

When selecting your board, consider the number of pins, the complexity of your project, and your specific needs (such as space or power consumption).

Installing the Arduino IDE

To start programming your Arduino, you'll need the **Arduino Integrated Development Environment (IDE)**. This software allows you to write code, upload it to your board, and monitor the output.

Here's how to install the Arduino IDE:

1. **Download the Arduino IDE**: Visit the official Arduino website (https://www.arduino.cc/en/software) and download the appropriate version for your operating system (Windows, macOS, or Linux).

2. **Install the IDE**: Follow the installation instructions for your operating system. The process is straightforward and typically involves running an installer and following the on-screen instructions.

3. **Connect Your Arduino Board**: Plug your Arduino board into your computer via a USB cable. The IDE will automatically detect the connected board.

4. **Select the Board and Port**: Open the Arduino IDE and go to the **Tools** menu. Select the correct Arduino board model from the **Board** submenu (for example, Arduino Uno) and choose the correct serial port (this may differ based on your operating system).

Once the IDE is set up and your board is connected, you're ready to start writing your first program!

Understanding the Basic Arduino Environment

The Arduino IDE is a simple and user-friendly platform. Here's a quick breakdown of the basic elements of the environment:

- **The Sketch**: In Arduino, programs are referred to as "sketches." A sketch consists of two main parts: the setup() function and the **loop()** function.
  - o **setup()**: This function runs once when the program starts. It's used to initialize variables, configure hardware, and set the initial conditions for your project.
  - o **loop()**: This function runs continuously after the setup() function. It's where you put the main code that makes your project run.
- **The Code Editor**: This is where you write and edit your sketches. It includes syntax highlighting, making it easier to spot errors in your code.
- **Serial Monitor**: The Serial Monitor is a debugging tool that allows you to communicate with your Arduino via

text. It's especially useful for checking sensor readings or troubleshooting.

Now that you have an understanding of the environment, you can start writing your first program!

Your First "Hello World" Project: Blinking an LED

The classic first project for any programming language is the "Hello World" project. In the case of Arduino, that's typically **blinking an LED**. This simple project will help you understand how to control outputs using the Arduino board.

Materials Needed:

- 1x Arduino board (e.g., Arduino Uno)
- 1x LED
- 1x 220-ohm resistor
- Breadboard and jumper wires

Steps:

1. **Circuit Setup**: Insert the LED into the breadboard. Connect the **longer leg (anode)** of the LED to pin 13

on the Arduino board and the **shorter leg (cathode)** to the GND (ground) pin on the Arduino through a 220-ohm resistor. The resistor is used to limit the current going through the LED, preventing it from burning out.

2. **Writing the Code**: Open the Arduino IDE, and in the editor, write the following code:

cpp

```
void setup() {
  pinMode(13, OUTPUT);  // Initialize digital pin
13 as an output.
}

void loop() {
  digitalWrite(13, HIGH);   // Turn the LED on.
  delay(1000);              // Wait for 1 second.
  digitalWrite(13, LOW);    // Turn the LED off.
  delay(1000);              // Wait for 1 second.
}
```

Explanation:

- In the setup() function, we initialize pin 13 as an output pin using the pinMode() function.
- In the loop() function, we turn the LED on (digitalWrite(13, HIGH)), wait for 1 second

(`delay(1000)`), turn the LED off(`digitalWrite(13,`
`LOW)`), and wait for another second.

3. **Upload the Code**: Click on the **Upload** button in the Arduino IDE. The code will be transferred to your Arduino board, and the LED should start blinking on and off every second.

With this simple "Hello World" project, you've successfully written, uploaded, and executed your first Arduino program! This basic exercise gives you a hands-on introduction to programming and controlling electronic components. In the next chapter, we'll start exploring more complex components, such as sensors and motors, that you can control with Arduino.

Stay tuned as we move further into the world of Arduino!

CHAPTER 3

THE ARDUINO PROGRAMMING LANGUAGE

In this chapter, we'll dive into the programming language that powers your Arduino projects. The Arduino programming language is based on C/C++, which is widely used for embedded systems and general programming. Don't worry if you're new to programming—this chapter is designed to be beginner-friendly, and we'll guide you through the essential concepts and syntax so you can start writing and understanding your own code.

Overview of the Arduino Programming Syntax

The Arduino programming language, while based on C/C++, is simplified for ease of use. The structure of an Arduino sketch consists of two main functions:

- **setup()**: This function runs once when the Arduino is powered on or reset. It is used to initialize variables, set pin modes, and configure libraries.

- **loop()**: This function runs repeatedly after setup() is executed. It contains the main code that makes your project operate continuously.

The code is written in plain text in the Arduino IDE. Each instruction is called a **statement**, and each statement ends with a semicolon (*;*). Here's an example of a basic Arduino sketch structure:

cpp

```cpp
void setup() {
  // Initialization code goes here
}

void loop() {
  // Repeated code goes here
}
```

Now that you have an overview of the basic structure, let's explore the building blocks of the language—variables, data types, and operators.

Variables, Data Types, and Operators

Variables

Variables are used to store information that can be accessed and modified by your program. They represent data values, such as numbers, text, or boolean values. Each variable in Arduino needs to have a **data type** to define what kind of data it holds.

Here's how you declare a variable:

cpp

```
int ledPin = 13; // Declare a variable named
ledPin of type int and assign it the value 13
```

Data Types

Here are some common data types used in Arduino programming:

- **int**: Used to store integers (whole numbers). Example: `int number = 5;`
- **float**: Used to store decimal numbers (floating-point numbers). Example: `float temperature = 23.5;`
- **char**: Used to store single characters. Example: `char grade = 'A';`
- **boolean**: Used to store a true/false value. Example: `boolean ledState = true;`

Operators

Operators are symbols that perform operations on variables and values. Some basic operators include:

- **Arithmetic operators**:
    - +: Addition
    - −: Subtraction
    - *: Multiplication
    - /: Division
    - %: Modulus (remainder of a division)

Example:

cpp

```
int a = 5;
int b = 3;
int result = a + b;  // result will be 8
```

- **Comparison operators**:
    - ==: Equal to
    - !=: Not equal to
    - <: Less than
    - >: Greater than
    - <=: Less than or equal to
    - >=: Greater than or equal to

Example:

cpp

```
if (a > b) {
  // If a is greater than b, this code will run
}
```

- **Logical operators**:
  - o `&&`: AND
  - o `||`: OR
  - o `!`: NOT

Example:

cpp

```
if (a > 0 && b < 5) {
  // Both conditions must be true
}
```

Now that you know how to work with variables and operators, let's look at how to control the flow of your program using functions and loops.

Understanding Functions and Loops

Functions

Functions in Arduino are blocks of code that perform a specific task. They help organize your code and make it reusable. There are two types of functions:

1. **Built-in functions**: These come with the Arduino environment. Examples include `pinMode()`, `digitalWrite()`, and `delay()`.
2. **Custom functions**: You can define your own functions to perform specific tasks.

Here's an example of a custom function:

cpp

```cpp
void blinkLED() {
  digitalWrite(13, HIGH); // Turn on LED
  delay(1000);            // Wait for 1 second
  digitalWrite(13, LOW);  // Turn off LED
  delay(1000);            // Wait for 1 second
}
```

In the above code, `blinkLED()` is a custom function that turns an LED on and off. To use it, you would simply call the function in your `loop()` or `setup()`:

cpp

```cpp
void loop() {
```

40

```cpp
blinkLED();   // Call the blinkLED function
}
```

Loops

Loops allow you to repeat a set of instructions multiple times. Arduino has two main types of loops:

- **for() loop**: Executes a block of code a specific number of times.

Example:

cpp

```cpp
for (int i = 0; i < 10; i++) {
  digitalWrite(13, HIGH);   // Turn LED on
  delay(500);                    // Wait for 0.5
seconds
  digitalWrite(13, LOW);    // Turn LED off
  delay(500);                    // Wait for 0.5
seconds
}
```

- **while() loop**: Executes a block of code as long as a specified condition is true.

Example:

cpp

```
while (true) {
  digitalWrite(13, HIGH);   // Turn LED on
  delay(500);                      // Wait for 0.5
seconds
  digitalWrite(13, LOW);    // Turn LED off
  delay(500);                      // Wait for 0.5
seconds
}
```

In this case, the `while()` loop will run indefinitely, making the LED blink forever.

Hands-On Coding Practice

Now that you understand the basic syntax, variables, operators, functions, and loops, it's time for some hands-on coding! Let's write a program that makes an LED blink with a pattern.

Materials Needed:

- Arduino board (e.g., Arduino Uno)
- LED
- 220-ohm resistor

- Breadboard and jumper wires

Steps:

1. **Circuit Setup**:
   - Connect the **longer leg (anode)** of the LED to pin 13 on the Arduino board.
   - Connect the **shorter leg (cathode)** to the GND pin through a 220-ohm resistor.

2. **Write the Code**: Open the Arduino IDE and write the following code:

cpp

```
void setup() {
  pinMode(13, OUTPUT);  // Set pin 13 as an output
}

void loop() {
  digitalWrite(13, HIGH);  // Turn LED on
  delay(500);                    // Wait for 0.5
seconds
  digitalWrite(13, LOW);   // Turn LED off
  delay(500);                    // Wait for 0.5
seconds
}
```

3. **Upload the Code**: Click the **Upload** button in the Arduino IDE. The LED will blink on and off at a half-second interval.

In this chapter, you've learned the basics of the Arduino programming language, including variables, data types, operators, functions, and loops. You've also written a hands-on project to blink an LED. As we move forward, we'll dive deeper into working with sensors and other components to expand your Arduino projects even further. Keep practicing, and don't be afraid to experiment with your own variations of the code!

CHAPTER 4

UNDERSTANDING ARDUINO INPUT AND OUTPUT

In this chapter, we will explore how Arduino interacts with the outside world. Arduino is designed to take inputs (like sensor data or user interaction) and produce outputs (like controlling LEDs, motors, or other devices). Understanding how Arduino communicates through its pins, and the concepts of voltage, current, and resistance, is crucial for building more advanced projects. By the end of this chapter, you'll be able to control electronic components through Arduino using both digital and analog pins.

How Arduino Communicates with the Outside World

Arduino interacts with the physical world through its **pins**. These pins can be configured to either receive input from sensors or send output to devices like LEDs, motors, or displays. There are two main types of pins on Arduino: **digital pins** and **analog pins**.

- **Digital Pins**: These pins can either read or send binary signals, which are either HIGH (1) or LOW (0). Digital pins are used for simple on/off operations.
- **Analog Pins**: These pins can read a range of values, from 0 to 1023 (in most cases), representing voltages between 0 and 5V. Analog pins are used for sensors that provide a variable output (like temperature sensors, potentiometers, or light sensors).

Understanding how to use both types of pins is fundamental to controlling devices and reading inputs on Arduino.

Using Digital and Analog Pins

Digital Pins

- **Digital Inputs**: When you use a digital pin to read input, it's usually in the form of a HIGH or LOW signal. For example, if you connect a button or a switch to a digital pin, you can check if the button is pressed (HIGH) or not pressed (LOW).
- **Digital Outputs**: When you use a digital pin to send output, you either turn the pin ON (HIGH) or OFF

(LOW). A common example is controlling an LED by turning it on or off.

Analog Pins

- **Analog Inputs**: Analog pins are used when you need to measure continuous changes, like reading the value from a temperature sensor or a light-dependent resistor (LDR). The input is mapped to a value between 0 and 1023, corresponding to a voltage range of 0 to 5V.

- **Analog Outputs**: Arduino boards don't have true analog outputs. However, you can use **PWM (Pulse Width Modulation)** on certain pins to simulate an analog output. PWM allows you to control the brightness of an LED or the speed of a motor by adjusting the duty cycle of the signal.

Understanding Voltage, Current, and Resistance

Before diving into practical projects, it's important to understand some basic electrical concepts: **voltage**, **current**, and **resistance**. These three elements are related and play a key role in how Arduino circuits work.

47

- **Voltage** (V) is the electrical potential difference between two points in a circuit. It pushes current through the circuit. Arduino typically works with 5V (though some boards may use 3.3V).

- **Current** (I) is the flow of electric charge through a conductor. It is measured in amperes (A). Arduino pins can handle a limited amount of current (usually 40mA per pin), so it's essential to use resistors and other components to ensure you don't exceed these limits.

- **Resistance** (R) is the opposition to the flow of current. It is measured in ohms (Ω). The relationship between voltage, current, and resistance is described by **Ohm's Law**:

$$V = I \times R$$

For example, if you have a 5V power supply and a resistor of 220 ohms, the current flowing through the circuit can be calculated as:

$$I = \frac{V}{R} = \frac{5V}{220 \, \Omega} \approx 0.023A \, (23mA)$$

In most projects, you'll use **resistors** to limit the current flowing through components like LEDs to prevent them from burning out.

Practical Project: Controlling an LED with a Button

Now that you have an understanding of Arduino input and output, it's time to put that knowledge to use in a practical project. In this project, we'll control an LED using a button. When you press the button, the LED will turn on, and when you release the button, the LED will turn off.

Materials Needed:

- 1x Arduino board (e.g., Arduino Uno)
- 1x LED
- 1x 220-ohm resistor
- 1x Pushbutton
- 1x 10k-ohm resistor (for the button)
- Breadboard and jumper wires

Steps:

1. **Circuit Setup**:

- o Insert the **LED** into the breadboard. Connect the **longer leg (anode)** to pin 13 on the Arduino board and the **shorter leg (cathode)** to GND through the 220-ohm resistor.
- o Connect one leg of the **pushbutton** to pin 7 on the Arduino and the other leg to GND.
- o Use the 10k-ohm resistor to connect the button leg going to pin 7 to 5V. This pull-up resistor ensures the button reads HIGH when not pressed and LOW when pressed.

2. **Write the Code**: Open the Arduino IDE and write the following code:

cpp

```cpp
int ledPin = 13;        // Pin where the LED is
connected
int buttonPin = 7;      // Pin where the button
is connected
int buttonState = 0;    // Variable to store the
button state

void setup() {
  pinMode(ledPin, OUTPUT);    // Set LED pin as
output
  pinMode(buttonPin, INPUT);  // Set button pin
as input
}
```

```
void loop() {
  buttonState = digitalRead(buttonPin);  // Read
the state of the button

  if (buttonState == HIGH) {  // If button is
pressed
    digitalWrite(ledPin, HIGH);  // Turn on the
LED
  } else {
    digitalWrite(ledPin, LOW);  // Turn off the
LED
  }
}
```

Explanation:

- In the `setup()` function, we configure pin 13 as an output (for the LED) and pin 7 as an input (for the button).
- In the `loop()` function, we constantly check the state of the button using `digitalRead()`. If the button is pressed (HIGH), the LED turns on; if not pressed (LOW), the LED turns off.

3. **Upload the Code**: Click the **Upload** button in the Arduino IDE. Once uploaded, press the button on the breadboard. The LED should light up when the button is pressed and turn off when the button is released.

51

Conclusion

In this chapter, you learned how Arduino communicates with the outside world through its digital and analog pins. You also learned about the fundamental electrical concepts of voltage, current, and resistance. By applying these concepts, you successfully built a project to control an LED with a button.

As you continue to explore Arduino, you'll see how you can use these same principles to create more complex and interactive projects. In the next chapter, we'll explore more advanced input and output devices, such as motors and displays, and how to integrate them into your projects. Keep experimenting and learning!

CHAPTER 5

SENSORS AND ACTUATORS

In this chapter, we'll explore sensors and actuators, which are essential components in many Arduino projects. Sensors allow Arduino to interact with the physical world by measuring properties like temperature, light, or motion. Actuators, on the other hand, enable Arduino to affect the physical world by controlling devices like motors, LEDs, or servos. We'll go over the most common sensors and actuators, how to interface with them, and provide practical projects that will help you get hands-on experience using them.

Overview of Common Sensors and Actuators

Sensors

Sensors are devices that detect changes in the environment and convert that information into electrical signals that Arduino can read. Sensors can be used to measure a wide range of variables, such as temperature, motion, light intensity, and more.

- **Light Dependent Resistor (LDR)**: An LDR is a type of sensor that detects light intensity. Its resistance decreases as the light intensity increases, and it can be used to measure light levels in your environment.
- **PIR Motion Sensor**: The Passive Infrared (PIR) sensor detects motion by sensing infrared radiation emitted by objects (like humans or animals). It is commonly used in motion detection systems.
- **Temperature Sensor (LM35 or DHT11)**: A temperature sensor measures the ambient temperature. The LM35 provides an analog output that corresponds to the temperature in Celsius, while the DHT11 provides both temperature and humidity data.

Actuators

Actuators are devices that perform actions based on the signals sent from the Arduino. They allow Arduino to control the environment by producing physical effects, such as turning on an LED, controlling a motor, or moving a robotic arm.

- **LEDs**: A Light Emitting Diode is a basic actuator that emits light when current flows through it. It can be used to indicate status or provide visual feedback in projects.
- **Motors**: Motors convert electrical energy into mechanical motion. There are different types, such as DC motors (for simple rotation), stepper motors (for precise positioning), and servo motors (for controlled angular movement).
- **Servos**: A servo motor is a small actuator that allows precise control over its angular position. It's commonly used in robotics, camera sliders, and other devices requiring controlled movement.

Interfacing with Temperature, Motion, and Light Sensors

Let's now look at how to interface these sensors with Arduino and make them work together to detect environmental conditions.

Interfacing with an LDR (Light Dependent Resistor)

The LDR is a simple sensor that changes its resistance based on the amount of light falling on it. It's typically used in light-sensitive applications like automatic streetlights or daylight sensors.

Wiring the LDR to Arduino:

1. **LDR**: Connect one end of the LDR to **5V** on the Arduino and the other end to an analog input pin (e.g., A0).
2. **Resistor**: Connect a 10k-ohm resistor between the LDR and **GND** to create a voltage divider circuit.

Code to Read LDR Values:

cpp

```cpp
int ldrPin = A0;   // LDR connected to analog pin A0
int ldrValue = 0;   // Variable to store the LDR value

void setup() {
  Serial.begin(9600);      //   Start   serial communication
}

void loop() {
  ldrValue = analogRead(ldrPin);  // Read the LDR value
  Serial.println(ldrValue);        // Print the value to the serial monitor
```

```
  delay(1000);                    // Wait for 1
second
}
```

This code reads the value from the LDR and prints it to the serial monitor. The LDR value will change based on the amount of light hitting it.

Interfacing with a PIR Motion Sensor

The PIR sensor detects motion by sensing changes in infrared radiation. It has two pins—**VCC** (for power) and **OUT** (for the signal), which outputs a HIGH signal when motion is detected.

Wiring the PIR Sensor to Arduino:

1. **PIR Sensor**: Connect the **VCC** pin to **5V**, the **GND** pin to **GND**, and the **OUT** pin to a digital input pin (e.g., pin 7).

Code to Detect Motion:

```cpp
cpp

int pirPin = 7;   // PIR sensor connected to pin
7
int pirState = 0; // Variable to store PIR state
```

```
void setup() {
  pinMode(pirPin, INPUT);   // Set the PIR sensor
pin as input
  Serial.begin(9600);              // Start serial
communication
}


void loop() {
  pirState = digitalRead(pirPin);   // Read the
PIR sensor state
  if (pirState == HIGH) {            // If motion
is detected
    Serial.println("Motion detected!");
  } else {
    Serial.println("No motion");
  }
  delay(1000);   // Wait for 1 second
}
```

This code detects motion and prints a message to the serial monitor whenever motion is detected.

Interfacing with a Temperature Sensor (LM35)

The LM35 is an analog temperature sensor that provides a voltage proportional to the temperature. It's simple to interface with and provides precise temperature readings.

Wiring the LM35 to Arduino:

1. **LM35**: Connect the **VCC** pin to **5V**, the **GND** pin to GND, and the **OUT** pin to an analog input pin (e.g., A1).

Code to Read Temperature:

cpp

```cpp
int tempPin = A1;     // LM35 connected to analog pin A1
float temperature = 0;  // Variable to store the temperature

void setup() {
  Serial.begin(9600);         //  Start   serial communication
}

void loop() {
  int tempReading = analogRead(tempPin);  // Read the analog value from LM35
  temperature = (tempReading * 5.0 * 100.0) / 1024.0;  // Convert reading to Celsius
  Serial.print("Temperature: ");
  Serial.print(temperature);     //  Print   the temperature
  Serial.println(" C");
  delay(1000);  // Wait for 1 second
```

}

This code converts the analog value from the LM35 into a temperature in Celsius and prints it to the serial monitor.

Practical Projects Using Sensors

Now that you understand how to interface with sensors, let's look at some practical projects that combine these sensors with Arduino.

Project 1: Automatic Night Light (Using LDR)

This project will use an LDR to automatically turn on an LED when the light level drops below a certain threshold (indicating it's getting dark).

Wiring:

- Connect the LDR circuit (as described earlier) to **A0**.
- Connect an LED to pin 13.

Code:

cpp

```
int ldrPin = A0;
int ledPin = 13;
int ldrValue = 0;
int threshold = 500;    // Set a threshold value
for darkness

void setup() {
  pinMode(ledPin, OUTPUT);
  Serial.begin(9600);
}

void loop() {
  ldrValue = analogRead(ldrPin);
  Serial.println(ldrValue);

  if (ldrValue < threshold) {  // If it's dark
    digitalWrite(ledPin, HIGH);   // Turn on the
LED
  } else {
    digitalWrite(ledPin, LOW);    // Turn off the
LED
  }
  delay(1000);
}
```

This project will automatically turn on the LED when the light level is below the threshold, simulating an automatic night light.

Project 2: Motion-Activated Alarm (Using PIR Sensor)

In this project, we will use a PIR sensor to activate an alarm when motion is detected.

Wiring:

- Connect the PIR sensor to pin 7 (as described earlier).
- Connect a buzzer to pin 8.

Code:

```cpp
cpp

int pirPin = 7;
int buzzerPin = 8;
int pirState = 0;

void setup() {
  pinMode(pirPin, INPUT);
  pinMode(buzzerPin, OUTPUT);
  Serial.begin(9600);
}

void loop() {
  pirState = digitalRead(pirPin);
  if (pirState == HIGH) {  // Motion detected
```

```
    digitalWrite(buzzerPin, HIGH);   // Sound the
alarm
    Serial.println("Motion detected!");
  } else {
    digitalWrite(buzzerPin, LOW);    // Turn off
the alarm
    Serial.println("No motion");
  }
  delay(1000);
}
```

This simple motion-activated alarm will sound the buzzer when the PIR sensor detects motion.

Conclusion

In this chapter, you learned about the most common sensors and actuators used with Arduino, how to interface with them, and how to read input from sensors like the LDR, PIR motion sensor, and temperature sensor. You also built practical projects that incorporated these components, like an automatic night light and a motion-activated alarm. Sensors and actuators are the foundation of many interactive and automated systems, and by understanding how to use them, you're opening up a world of possibilities for your Arduino projects.

CHAPTER 6

USING MOTORS WITH ARDUINO

Motors are essential components in robotics and automation, allowing your Arduino projects to move and interact with the physical world. In this chapter, we'll explore the three most common types of motors—DC motors, stepper motors, and servo motors—along with how to control them using Arduino. We'll also walk through a practical project: building a simple motorized car.

Types of Motors: DC, Stepper, and Servo

DC Motors

DC motors are one of the simplest types of motors. They convert electrical energy into rotational motion using direct current (DC) power. DC motors are commonly used for simple movement tasks, like driving wheels on a robot or controlling the speed of a fan.

- **Characteristics**:

65

- o Simple to control with basic ON/OFF switches or variable speeds.
- o Can rotate continuously in one direction.
- o Can be controlled using Pulse Width Modulation (PWM) for speed control.

Stepper Motors

Stepper motors move in discrete steps, allowing for precise control over position. Unlike DC motors, which rotate continuously, stepper motors move by a specific angle with each pulse of current. This makes them ideal for applications that require precise positioning, such as in 3D printers, CNC machines, or robotic arms.

- **Characteristics**:
    - o Moves in precise increments (steps).
    - o No need for external encoders.
    - o Suitable for applications requiring accuracy and controlled positioning.

Servo Motors

Servo motors are a type of motor used for precise position control, but unlike stepper motors, they are designed to rotate within a limited range (usually 0-180 degrees). Servo motors are widely used in applications like steering in robots, pan-and-tilt camera systems, and in robotics for controlled, precise movements.

- **Characteristics**:
  - Controlled by Pulse Width Modulation (PWM) signals.
  - Typically rotates between 0 and 180 degrees.
  - Ideal for applications where precise position control is needed.

How to Control Motors Using Arduino

Each type of motor has its unique control method, and you'll need different components to control them effectively with Arduino. Let's go over how to control DC motors, stepper motors, and servo motors using Arduino.

Controlling a DC Motor with Arduino

DC motors can be controlled using an **H-Bridge** motor driver, which allows the motor to rotate in both directions and control its speed. One common motor driver is the **L298N**.

Materials Needed:

- DC motor
- L298N motor driver
- Arduino board
- External power supply (for the motor)
- Jumper wires

Wiring:

1. Connect the motor terminals to the motor output pins on the L298N.
2. Connect the **ENA** pin to 5V to enable motor control.
3. Connect the **IN1** and **IN2** pins to Arduino pins (e.g., pin 9 and pin 10) for controlling the motor direction.
4. Connect the **GND** pin on the motor driver to GND on Arduino.
5. Power the motor through the **VCC** pin on the L298N using an external power source.

Code to Control DC Motor:

cpp

```cpp
int motorPin1 = 9;  // Pin to control the motor
direction
int motorPin2 = 10; // Pin to control the motor
direction
```

```
void setup() {
  pinMode(motorPin1, OUTPUT);   // Set motor pins
as output
  pinMode(motorPin2, OUTPUT);   // Set motor pins
as output
}


void loop() {
  digitalWrite(motorPin1,  HIGH);      // Motor
rotates in one direction
  digitalWrite(motorPin2, LOW);
  delay(2000);  // Run motor for 2 seconds

  digitalWrite(motorPin1,  LOW);       // Motor
rotates in the opposite direction
  digitalWrite(motorPin2, HIGH);
  delay(2000);  // Run motor for 2 seconds
}
```

This code will make the motor rotate in one direction for 2 seconds, then reverse for another 2 seconds.

Controlling a Stepper Motor with Arduino

Step motors require a different type of control to move precisely. The most common method is to use a stepper motor driver, such as the **A4988** or **ULN2003**.

Materials Needed:

- Stepper motor (e.g., 28BYJ-48)
- Stepper motor driver (e.g., ULN2003)
- Arduino board
- Jumper wires

Wiring:

1. Connect the four wires of the stepper motor to the driver.
2. Connect the motor driver to the Arduino (IN1, IN2, IN3, IN4 pins to Arduino digital pins).
3. Connect the **VCC** and **GND** of the motor driver to the **5V** and **GND** on the Arduino.

Code to Control Stepper Motor:

cpp

```cpp
#include <Stepper.h>

const int stepsPerRevolution = 2048;   // Number
of steps for one full revolution
Stepper myStepper(stepsPerRevolution, 8, 9, 10,
11);  // Pin 8-11 for stepper motor control

void setup() {
  myStepper.setSpeed(15);  // Set motor speed to
15 RPM
```

```
}

void loop() {
  myStepper.step(stepsPerRevolution);    // Make
one full revolution
  delay(2000);  // Wait for 2 seconds
  myStepper.step(-stepsPerRevolution);        //
Reverse one full revolution
  delay(2000);  // Wait for 2 seconds
}
```

This code will rotate the stepper motor one full revolution clockwise, pause, then reverse the direction for another full revolution.

Controlling a Servo Motor with Arduino

Servo motors are easy to control using Arduino. You only need a PWM signal to set the angle of the motor. The **Servo library** in Arduino makes controlling servos simple.

Materials Needed:

- Servo motor
- Arduino board
- Jumper wires

Wiring:

71

1. Connect the servo signal pin to any PWM-capable pin on Arduino (e.g., pin 9).
2. Connect the **VCC** pin of the servo to 5V on the Arduino and the **GND** pin to GND.

Code to Control Servo Motor:

cpp

```
#include <Servo.h>

Servo myServo;   // Create a Servo object
int angle = 0;   // Initial angle for the servo

void setup() {
  myServo.attach(9);   // Attach the servo to pin
9
}

void loop() {
  for (angle = 0; angle <= 180; angle++) {   //
Sweep from 0 to 180 degrees
    myServo.write(angle);
    delay(15);   // Wait for the servo to reach
the position
  }
  for (angle = 180; angle >= 0; angle--) {   //
Sweep back from 180 to 0 degrees
    myServo.write(angle);
```

```
   delay(15);
  }
}
```

This code will make the servo motor sweep back and forth between 0 and 180 degrees.

Practical Project: Building a Simple Motorized Car

Now that we understand how to control different types of motors, let's apply that knowledge in a simple project: building a motorized car using DC motors. In this project, you'll create a car that moves forward and backward using a simple Arduino setup.

Materials Needed:

- 2x DC motors
- L298N motor driver
- Arduino board
- 2x wheels
- Chassis (can be a simple cardboard or plastic base)
- Jumper wires
- 9V battery (for power)
- Battery holder

Steps:

1. **Wiring the Motors**:
    o Connect the two DC motors to the motor output pins on the L298N motor driver.
    o Connect the motor driver pins to Arduino (for example, pin 9 and pin 10 for motor direction control).
    o Power the motors with a 9V battery connected to the **VCC** pin on the L298N.

2. **Assembling the Car**:
    o Attach the wheels to the motors.
    o Secure the motors and Arduino to the chassis.
    o Make sure the wires are connected to the correct pins for controlling the motors.

3. **Code to Control the Motors**:

cpp

```
int motorPin1 = 9;  // Motor 1 direction pin
int motorPin2 = 10; // Motor 2 direction pin
int motorPin3 = 11; // Motor 1 speed control pin
(PWM)
int motorPin4 = 12; // Motor 2 speed control pin
(PWM)

void setup() {
```

```
  pinMode(motorPin1,  OUTPUT);    // Set motor
control pins as output
  pinMode(motorPin2, OUTPUT);
  pinMode(motorPin3, OUTPUT);
  pinMode(motorPin4, OUTPUT);
}

void loop() {
  // Move forward
  digitalWrite(motorPin1, HIGH);
  digitalWrite(motorPin2, LOW);
  analogWrite(motorPin3, 255);  // Full speed
  analogWrite(motorPin4, 255);  // Full speed
  delay(2000);  // Move forward for 2 seconds

  // Move backward
  digitalWrite(motorPin1, LOW);
  digitalWrite(motorPin2, HIGH);
  analogWrite(motorPin3, 255);
  analogWrite(motorPin4, 255);
  delay(2000);  // Move backward for 2 seconds
}
```

This code makes the motorized car move forward for 2 seconds, then backward for 2 seconds in a loop.

Conclusion

In this chapter, you learned how to control different types of motors using Arduino—DC motors, stepper motors, and servo motors. You also completed a practical project by building a simple motorized car, combining your understanding of motor control with Arduino programming. Motors are fundamental components in robotics and automation, and now you have the skills to create your own mobile projects. In the next chapter, we'll explore more advanced topics and build upon the skills you've developed here. Happy building!

CHAPTER 8

WORKING WITH WI-FI AND BLUETOOTH

In this chapter, we'll explore wireless communication with Arduino, focusing on two popular communication technologies: **Wi-Fi** and **Bluetooth**. These technologies allow your Arduino projects to interact with other devices, such as smartphones, computers, or other Arduinos, without the need for physical cables. By the end of this chapter, you'll be able to control an LED via a smartphone using both Wi-Fi and Bluetooth.

Introduction to Wireless Communication

Wireless communication allows devices to communicate over short or long distances without the need for wires. There are various methods to achieve this, but in Arduino projects, the most common wireless communication modules are:

- **Wi-Fi**: This allows Arduino to connect to the internet or a local network, enabling communication with web servers, apps, or other devices connected to the same network.

- **Bluetooth**: This is a short-range communication technology used for simple device-to-device communication. It is ideal for mobile app-controlled projects, such as controlling robots or home automation systems.

Let's now dive into how you can implement both Wi-Fi and Bluetooth communication with Arduino using two popular modules: **ESP8266** for Wi-Fi and **HC-05** for Bluetooth.

Setting up Wi-Fi with the ESP8266

The **ESP8266** is a low-cost Wi-Fi module that can be easily interfaced with Arduino to enable wireless communication. It can connect your Arduino to the internet or a local Wi-Fi network, allowing you to control devices remotely or send/receive data over the internet.

Materials Needed:

- ESP8266 Wi-Fi module

- Arduino board (e.g., Arduino Uno)
- Jumper wires
- Breadboard (optional)
- External power supply for ESP8266 (if needed)

Wiring the ESP8266:

1. Connect the **TX** pin of the ESP8266 to the **RX** pin of the Arduino (Pin 0).
2. Connect the **RX** pin of the ESP8266 to the **TX** pin of the Arduino (Pin 1).
3. Connect **GND** and **VCC** to GND and 3.3V on Arduino, respectively (note: the ESP8266 requires 3.3V, not 5V).
4. If the ESP8266 requires more power, you may need an external 3.3V power supply.

Code to Connect to Wi-Fi:

To get started, we'll first program the Arduino to connect to a Wi-Fi network using the ESP8266 module. We will use the **SoftwareSerial** library to communicate with the ESP8266 through pins 0 and 1.

cpp

```cpp
#include <SoftwareSerial.h>
```

```
SoftwareSerial espSerial(2, 3);  // RX, TX pins
for ESP8266 communication
String ssid = "your_network_name";   // Wi-Fi
network name
String password = "your_password";   // Wi-Fi
password

void setup() {
  Serial.begin(9600);              // Start serial
communication
  espSerial.begin(115200);                 // Start
communication with ESP8266

  Serial.println("Connecting to Wi-Fi...");

  // Send AT commands to ESP8266 to connect to
the Wi-Fi network
  espSerial.print("AT+CWJAP=\"" + ssid + "\",\""
+ password + "\"\r\n");
  delay(5000);     // Wait for connection to
complete

  // Check if the connection was successful
  if (espSerial.available()) {
    Serial.println(espSerial.readString());
  } else {
    Serial.println("Connection failed!");
  }
}
```

```
void loop() {
  // Main loop does nothing here, just keeps the
connection alive
}
```

Explanation:

- The **SoftwareSerial** library is used to communicate with the ESP8266 module on pins 2 and 3.
- The code sends **AT commands** to the ESP8266 to connect to a Wi-Fi network. You'll need to replace `your_network_name` and `your_password` with your actual Wi-Fi credentials.
- Once connected, you can expand this code to communicate with online services or control devices remotely.

Bluetooth Communication with HC-05

The **HC-05** is a popular Bluetooth module for Arduino projects. It allows your Arduino to communicate wirelessly with smartphones or other Bluetooth-enabled devices. You can use Bluetooth to control devices or exchange data with mobile applications.

Materials Needed:

- HC-05 Bluetooth module
- Arduino board (e.g., Arduino Uno)
- Jumper wires
- Smartphone with Bluetooth capability

Wiring the HC-05:

1. Connect the **TX** pin of the HC-05 to **RX** pin 0 of the Arduino.
2. Connect the **RX** pin of the HC-05 to **TX** pin 1 of the Arduino.
3. Connect **VCC** and **GND** of the HC-05 to **5V** and **GND** of Arduino, respectively.

Code to Control LED via Bluetooth:

Now that the HC-05 is set up, let's control an LED using Bluetooth. We'll send commands from a smartphone app (like a Bluetooth terminal app) to control the LED.

cpp

```cpp
int ledPin = 13;  // Pin where LED is connected
char receivedChar;  // Variable to store the
received Bluetooth data
```

```
void setup() {
  Serial.begin(9600);        //   Start    serial
communication for Bluetooth
  pinMode(ledPin, OUTPUT);   // Set LED pin as
output
}

void loop() {
  if (Serial.available() > 0) {
    receivedChar = Serial.read();   // Read the
Bluetooth data

    if (receivedChar == '1') {
      digitalWrite(ledPin, HIGH);  // Turn on LED
if '1' is received
    } else if (receivedChar == '0') {
      digitalWrite(ledPin, LOW);  // Turn off LED
if '0' is received
    }
  }
}
```

Explanation:

- This code listens for incoming data from the HC-05
  module. If it receives the character 1, it turns on the LED;
  if it receives 0, it turns the LED off.
- You can use a Bluetooth terminal app on your smartphone
  to send these characters to the Arduino via the HC-05.

Practical Project: Controlling an LED via Smartphone

Now that we've covered both Wi-Fi and Bluetooth, let's put it all together in a project where you can control an LED using a smartphone.

Project 1: Controlling LED via Wi-Fi (Using ESP8266)

This project will use the ESP8266 Wi-Fi module to control an LED via a smartphone's web browser.

Materials Needed:

- ESP8266 Wi-Fi module
- Arduino board
- LED
- 220-ohm resistor
- Jumper wires

Steps:

1. Set up the ESP8266 to connect to your Wi-Fi network (as shown earlier).

2. Modify the code to create a simple web server on the ESP8266 to toggle the LED via a browser.

cpp

```cpp
#include <ESP8266WiFi.h>

const char* ssid = "your_network_name";   // Wi-
Fi SSID
const char* password = "your_password";   // Wi-
Fi password

WiFiServer server(80);   // Web server on port 80
int ledPin = 13;         // Pin for the LED

void setup() {
  Serial.begin(115200);
  pinMode(ledPin, OUTPUT);

  // Connect to Wi-Fi
  WiFi.begin(ssid, password);
  while (WiFi.status() != WL_CONNECTED) {
    delay(1000);
    Serial.print(".");
  }
  Serial.println("Connected to Wi-Fi");

  // Start the server
  server.begin();
```

```
}

void loop() {
  WiFiClient client = server.available();   //
Check for incoming client
  if (client) {
    String               request               =
client.readStringUntil('\r');
    client.flush();

    // Control the LED based on the HTTP request
    if (request.indexOf("/led/on") != -1) {
      digitalWrite(ledPin, HIGH);
    } else if (request.indexOf("/led/off") != -
1) {
      digitalWrite(ledPin, LOW);
    }

    // Send a simple HTML response
    client.print("HTTP/1.1 200 OK\n");
    client.print("Content-Type: text/html\n");
    client.print("Connection: close\n\n");
    client.print("<html><body><h1>LED
Control</h1>");
    client.print("<a  href=\"/led/on\">Turn  LED
On</a><br>");
    client.print("<a  href=\"/led/off\">Turn  LED
Off</a><br>");
    client.print("</body></html>");
```

```
    }
}
```

Explanation:

- This code sets up a simple web server on the ESP8266. When a user accesses the web page, they can click links to turn the LED on or off.
- The ESP8266 serves the HTML page and listens for requests like `/led/on` or `/led/off` to control the LED.

Project 2: Controlling LED via Bluetooth (Using HC-05)

For the Bluetooth version, you'll control the LED from a Bluetooth terminal app on your smartphone.

Materials Needed:

- HC-05 Bluetooth module
- Arduino board
- LED
- 220-ohm resistor
- Jumper wires

Steps:

1. Set up the HC-05 module (as shown earlier).

2. Upload the code to the Arduino.

3. Use a Bluetooth terminal app to send 1 to turn the LED on and 0 to turn it off.

Conclusion

In this chapter, you've learned how to use wireless communication technologies like **Wi-Fi** and **Bluetooth** with Arduino. We covered the setup and use of the **ESP8266** for Wi-Fi connectivity and the **HC-05** Bluetooth module for device communication. You also completed practical projects where you controlled an LED via smartphone using both Wi-Fi and Bluetooth. These wireless capabilities open up a wide range of possibilities for building remote control systems, IoT devices, and more. Keep experimenting and integrating wireless communication into your Arduino projects!

CHAPTER 9

REAL-TIME CLOCK (RTC) WITH ARDUINO

In this chapter, we'll explore how to use a **Real-Time Clock (RTC)** module with Arduino. RTC modules are essential for projects that need to keep track of time, even when the power is turned off. They maintain accurate time and date through a built-in battery. We'll discuss how to interface an RTC with Arduino, how it works, and build a practical project: creating a real-time clock and calendar.

Understanding Real-Time Clocks and Their Importance

A **Real-Time Clock (RTC)** is a specialized clock designed to keep track of the current time and date. Unlike the Arduino's built-in clock (which resets every time the power is turned off), an RTC has a small battery that allows it to continue keeping time even when the system is powered down. This makes RTCs an ideal solution for projects like clocks, timers, and data logging systems that require accurate timekeeping.

Key Features of an RTC:

- **Keeps accurate time**: RTCs can maintain accurate time down to the second.
- **Battery-backed**: RTCs come with a small backup battery (usually a coin cell) that keeps them running when the Arduino is powered off.
- **Simple communication with Arduino**: RTC modules commonly use I2C or SPI communication to interact with the Arduino, making them easy to interface.

How to Interface an RTC Module with Arduino

One of the most popular RTC modules used in Arduino projects is the **DS3231**, which communicates with Arduino via I2C. It provides both time and date information and is highly accurate.

Materials Needed:

- Arduino board (e.g., Arduino Uno)
- DS3231 RTC module

- Jumper wires
- Breadboard (optional)

Wiring the DS3231 RTC Module to Arduino:

The DS3231 module uses **I2C** for communication, so it requires only four connections to the Arduino:

1. **VCC** to **5V** on Arduino.
2. **GND** to **GND** on Arduino.
3. **SDA** to **A4** on Arduino (for Uno).
4. **SCL** to **A5** on Arduino (for Uno).

If you're using a different Arduino model, make sure to connect the SDA and SCL pins to the appropriate pins for I2C communication.

Installing the RTC Library:

To interface with the DS3231 module, you need a library that simplifies communication. The **RTClib** library is commonly used for this purpose. You can install it from the Arduino Library Manager:

1. Go to **Sketch → Include Library → Manage Libraries**.
2. Search for **RTClib** and install it.

Code to Interface with the DS3231 RTC Module

Once the hardware is set up and the library is installed, you can start coding. Here's a simple example of how to read the current time from the DS3231 RTC module and print it to the serial monitor.

cpp

```cpp
#include <Wire.h>
#include <RTClib.h>

RTC_DS3231 rtc;    // Create an instance of the
RTC_DS3231 class

void setup() {
  Serial.begin(9600);         //    Start    serial
communication
  Wire.begin();  // Initialize I2C communication

  if (!rtc.begin()) {
    Serial.println("Couldn't find RTC");
    while (1);  // Stop if RTC is not found
  }

  if (rtc.lostPower()) {
```

```
    Serial.println("RTC lost power, setting the
time!");
    // Set the time to a default value (YYYY, MM,
DD, HH, MM, SS)
    rtc.adjust(DateTime(F(__DATE__),
F(__TIME__)));  // Sets the RTC to the compile
time
  }
}


void loop() {
  DateTime now = rtc.now();  // Get the current
date and time

  Serial.print("Date: ");
  Serial.print(now.year(), DEC);  // Print year
  Serial.print('/');
  Serial.print(now.month(), DEC);  // Print month
  Serial.print('/');
  Serial.print(now.day(), DEC);  // Print day
  Serial.print(" ");
  Serial.print("Time: ");
  Serial.print(now.hour(), DEC);  // Print hour
  Serial.print(':');
  Serial.print(now.minute(), DEC);    // Print
minute
  Serial.print(':');
  Serial.print(now.second(), DEC);    // Print
second
```

```
Serial.println();

delay(1000);   // Wait for 1 second
}
```

Explanation:

- We include the **Wire.h** and **RTClib.h** libraries to handle I2C communication and RTC functionality.
- In the `setup()` function, we check if the RTC is connected using `rtc.begin()`. If the RTC has lost power (e.g., the battery is removed), the code sets the time to the Arduino sketch's compile time.
- In the `loop()` function, we continuously read the current time using `rtc.now()` and print it to the serial monitor every second.

Practical Project: Creating a Real-Time Clock and Calendar

Now that you can read the current time from the RTC, let's create a practical project—a simple real-time clock and calendar display. We will use an LCD display to show the time and date, making it easy to view.

Materials Needed:

- Arduino board (e.g., Arduino Uno)
- DS3231 RTC module
- 16x2 LCD display (with I2C interface)
- Jumper wires
- Breadboard (optional)

Wiring the Components:

1. **RTC Module (DS3231)**: Connect the **VCC**, **GND**, **SDA**, and **SCL** pins as described earlier.
2. **LCD Display**: If your LCD has an I2C interface:
   - Connect **VCC** to **5V** on Arduino.
   - Connect **GND** to **GND** on Arduino.
   - Connect **SDA** to **A4** on Arduino.
   - Connect **SCL** to **A5** on Arduino.

Code to Display Time and Date on LCD:

cpp

```cpp
#include <Wire.h>
#include <RTClib.h>
#include <LiquidCrystal_I2C.h>

// Create instances of the RTC and LCD
RTC_DS3231 rtc;
```

```
LiquidCrystal_I2C lcd(0x27, 16, 2);    // I2C
address, width, height

void setup() {
  Serial.begin(9600);
  lcd.begin(16, 2);  // Initialize the LCD
  lcd.backlight();   // Turn on the LCD backlight
  Wire.begin();              // Initialize I2C
communication

  if (!rtc.begin()) {
    Serial.println("Couldn't find RTC");
    while (1);
  }

  if (rtc.lostPower()) {
    Serial.println("RTC lost power, setting the
time!");
    rtc.adjust(DateTime(F(__DATE__),
F(__TIME__)));
  }

  lcd.print("Real-Time Clock");    // Display
header
  delay(2000);  // Wait for 2 seconds
}

void loop() {
```

```
DateTime now = rtc.now();  // Get current date
and time

  // Display time
  lcd.setCursor(0, 0);    // Set cursor to the
first row
  lcd.print(now.hour(), DEC);
  lcd.print(':');
  lcd.print(now.minute(), DEC);
  lcd.print(':');
  lcd.print(now.second(), DEC);

  // Display date
  lcd.setCursor(0, 1);    // Set cursor to the
second row
  lcd.print(now.month(), DEC);
  lcd.print('/');
  lcd.print(now.day(), DEC);
  lcd.print('/');
  lcd.print(now.year(), DEC);

  delay(1000);  // Update every second
}
```

Explanation:

- In the setup() function, we initialize both the RTC and the LCD display. The LCD is used to show the current time and date in a readable format.

97

- In the `loop()`, the current time and date are continuously updated and displayed on the LCD every second.

Conclusion

In this chapter, you learned how to interface with a Real-Time Clock (RTC) module using the DS3231 and Arduino. We covered how to read the current time, set the time if the RTC loses power, and display the time and date on an LCD screen. RTC modules are invaluable for projects that require precise timekeeping, such as clocks, data logging, and scheduling systems. By understanding how to use the DS3231, you're now equipped to create time-sensitive projects that retain accuracy even when the system is powered off. Keep exploring and experimenting with RTCs to build even more advanced time-based projects!

CHAPTER 10

ARDUINO AND SOUND

Sound plays a crucial role in many Arduino projects, from simple notifications to complex music generation. In this chapter, we'll explore how to use **buzzers** and **speakers** with Arduino to generate sound. We'll learn how to generate various frequencies and tones, and we'll also build a practical project—a simple alarm system—using sound. By the end of this chapter, you'll have a solid foundation for adding sound to your future Arduino projects.

Using Buzzers and Speakers with Arduino

Buzzers

A **buzzer** is a simple electronic component that emits sound when voltage is applied to it. There are two main types of buzzers used with Arduino:

- **Active Buzzers**: These buzzers generate sound when power is applied. They don't require a signal to control the pitch, and they simply turn on and off.

- **Passive Buzzers**: These buzzers require a signal to control the pitch of the sound. By changing the frequency of the signal sent to a passive buzzer, you can generate different tones.

Speakers

A **speaker** can also be used to produce sound with Arduino. A speaker requires an audio signal, usually in the form of a pulse-width modulation (PWM) signal. Arduino can generate various frequencies by controlling the timing of the PWM signal sent to the speaker, allowing you to create music or alarms.

For most simple projects, an active buzzer is easier to use because it only requires a simple on/off signal. However, if you want more control over the sound, such as generating different tones or melodies, you'll use a passive buzzer or a speaker.

Generating Sound Frequencies and Tones

Arduino can generate sounds by creating a square wave signal at a specific frequency. The **tone()** function allows you to generate tones on a specified pin, while the **noTone()** function stops the sound.

Tone() Function

The **tone()** function allows you to generate a tone with a specified frequency on a given pin. Here's the basic syntax:

cpp

```
tone(pin, frequency);
```

- **pin**: The Arduino pin to which the buzzer or speaker is connected.
- **frequency**: The frequency of the tone in Hertz (Hz). Common tones include 440 Hz (A4 note) or 1000 Hz (higher pitch).

You can also use the **duration** parameter to specify how long the tone should last:

cpp

```
tone(pin, frequency, duration);
```

NoTone() Function

The **noTone()** function stops the sound on the specified pin:

```cpp
noTone(pin);
```

This is useful when you want to stop a tone after it has played for a certain amount of time.

Practical Project: Creating a Simple Alarm System

In this project, we'll create a simple alarm system that triggers a buzzer when motion is detected. The system will use a **PIR motion sensor** to detect movement and an **active buzzer** to sound the alarm. This project will help you understand how to generate sound in response to events in your environment.

Materials Needed:

- Arduino board (e.g., Arduino Uno)
- PIR motion sensor
- Active buzzer
- Jumper wires
- Breadboard (optional)

Wiring the Components:

1. **PIR Motion Sensor**:
   - ○ Connect the **VCC** pin to **5V** on the Arduino.
   - ○ Connect the **GND** pin to **GND** on the Arduino.
   - ○ Connect the **OUT** pin to a digital input pin on Arduino (e.g., pin 7).
2. **Active Buzzer**:
   - ○ Connect the **positive (longer leg)** of the buzzer to a digital output pin on Arduino (e.g., pin 8).
   - ○ Connect the **negative (shorter leg)** to **GND** on Arduino.

Code to Control the Buzzer with PIR Motion Sensor:

cpp

```
int pirPin = 7;   // Pin connected to PIR motion
sensor
int buzzerPin = 8;   // Pin connected to active
buzzer
int pirState = 0;  // Variable to store PIR sensor
state

void setup() {
  pinMode(pirPin, INPUT);   // Set PIR sensor pin
as input
  pinMode(buzzerPin, OUTPUT);   // Set buzzer pin
as output
```

```
  Serial.begin(9600);          //   Start   serial
communication for debugging
}


void loop() {
  pirState = digitalRead(pirPin);   // Read the
state of the PIR sensor

  if (pirState == HIGH) {   // If motion is
detected
    Serial.println("Motion detected! Activating
alarm...");
    tone(buzzerPin, 1000);   // Activate buzzer
with a 1000 Hz tone
  } else {
    Serial.println("No motion detected.");
    noTone(buzzerPin);   // Deactivate buzzer
  }


  delay(100);   // Wait for a short moment before
checking again
}
```

Explanation:

- The **pirPin** reads the state of the PIR sensor. When
  motion is detected, the PIR sensor outputs a HIGH signal.

- When motion is detected, the **tone()** function generates a 1000 Hz sound on the buzzer. When no motion is detected, the **noTone()** function stops the sound.
- The `Serial.print()` function helps us see the motion status in the serial monitor for debugging.

Enhancing the Alarm System with Multiple Tones

You can enhance the alarm system by adding different sounds for various situations. For example, you could make the buzzer emit a short high-pitched sound when motion is first detected and then a lower-pitched sound after a few seconds.

Code to Create Multiple Tones:

```cpp
cpp

int pirPin = 7;   // Pin connected to PIR motion
sensor
int buzzerPin = 8;   // Pin connected to active
buzzer
int pirState = 0;  // Variable to store PIR sensor
state

void setup() {
```

```
  pinMode(pirPin, INPUT);   // Set PIR sensor pin
as input
  pinMode(buzzerPin, OUTPUT);   // Set buzzer pin
as output
  Serial.begin(9600);          //   Start   serial
communication for debugging
}


void loop() {
  pirState = digitalRead(pirPin);   // Read the
state of the PIR sensor

  if (pirState == HIGH) {   // If motion is
detected
    Serial.println("Motion detected! Activating
alarm...");
    tone(buzzerPin, 1000);  // First, emit a 1000
Hz tone
    delay(1000);  // Wait for 1 second
    tone(buzzerPin, 500);   // Change the tone to
500 Hz
    delay(1000);  // Wait for another second
  } else {
    Serial.println("No motion detected.");
    noTone(buzzerPin);  // Deactivate buzzer
  }

  delay(100);  // Wait for a short moment before
checking again
```

}

Explanation:

- After detecting motion, the system emits a high-pitched sound at 1000 Hz for 1 second, then changes to a lower pitch at 500 Hz for another second.
- The **delay()** function controls how long each tone lasts.

Conclusion

In this chapter, we explored how to generate sound using Arduino by working with buzzers and speakers. We learned how to create different frequencies and tones using the **tone()** function and how to stop sounds using **noTone()**. We also built a practical project—a simple alarm system—that triggers a buzzer when motion is detected. Sound is a powerful way to enhance your Arduino projects, and with buzzers and speakers, you can create alerts, alarms, music, and much more. Keep experimenting with sound and consider adding it to your future Arduino projects!

CHAPTER 11

ADVANCED INPUTS: KEYPADS AND TOUCH SCREENS

In this chapter, we'll delve into advanced input methods, focusing on **matrix keypads** and **capacitive touch screens**. These input devices allow for more sophisticated and user-friendly control of Arduino projects. We will learn how to interface with matrix keypads, understand the principles of capacitive touch screens, and work on a practical project—a keypad-controlled door lock.

Working with Matrix Keypads

A **matrix keypad** is a type of keypad that consists of a grid of buttons arranged in rows and columns. Matrix keypads are often used for applications where a user needs to input data, such as security systems or interactive control panels. They are more compact and use fewer pins compared to traditional keypads.

How a Matrix Keypad Works

A typical matrix keypad is composed of buttons arranged in a grid of rows and columns. When a key is pressed, it connects one row to one column, creating a unique connection that the Arduino can detect. This method allows you to detect key presses using just a few pins on the Arduino instead of dedicating a pin to each button.

- **Rows**: The horizontal lines of buttons.
- **Columns**: The vertical lines of buttons.

The Arduino detects which key is pressed by scanning the rows and columns, using a process called **keypad scanning**.

Materials Needed:

- 4x4 Matrix Keypad
- Arduino board (e.g., Arduino Uno)
- Jumper wires

Wiring the Matrix Keypad:

1. Connect the 4 rows and 4 columns of the keypad to 8 digital pins on the Arduino.
2. Use the **Keypad** library, which simplifies the process of scanning the keypad and detecting key presses.

Code to Interface with Matrix Keypad:

First, you'll need to install the **Keypad** library. To install the library:

1. Go to **Sketch → Include Library → Manage Libraries**.
2. Search for **Keypad** and install it.

Here's an example code to detect key presses on a 4x4 matrix keypad:

cpp

```cpp
#include <Keypad.h>

// Define the keypad layout
const byte ROW_NUM    = 4;   // Four rows
const byte COLUMN_NUM = 4;   // Four columns
char keys[ROW_NUM][COLUMN_NUM] = {
  {'1','2','3','A'},
  {'4','5','6','B'},
  {'7','8','9','C'},
  {'*','0','#','D'}
};
byte pin_rows[ROW_NUM] = {9, 8, 7, 6}; // Connect
to the row pinouts
byte pin_column[COLUMN_NUM] = {5, 4, 3, 2}; //
Connect to the column pinouts

Keypad    keypad    =    Keypad(makeKeymap(keys),
pin_rows, pin_column, ROW_NUM, COLUMN_NUM);
```

```
void setup() {
  Serial.begin(9600);
}


void loop() {
  char key = keypad.getKey();
  if (key) {
    Serial.print("You pressed: ");
    Serial.println(key);
  }
}
```

Explanation:

- The **Keypad** library is used to manage the key matrix and simplify the scanning process.
- The code continuously checks for key presses, and when a key is pressed, it prints the key to the serial monitor.

Understanding Capacitive Touch Screens

A **capacitive touch screen** is a type of input device that detects touch by measuring the change in the electrical field. When your finger touches the screen, it changes the capacitance at the point of contact, which the screen detects

111

and processes. Capacitive touch screens are commonly used in smartphones, tablets, and other modern touch-based devices.

How a Capacitive Touch Screen Works

- **Capacitance**: A capacitive touch screen works by measuring changes in the capacitance when a conductive object (like your finger) touches the screen.
- **Touch Detection**: The touch screen is divided into a grid of capacitive sensors that can detect the location of the touch. The Arduino can then interpret these changes and determine which part of the screen was touched.

Materials Needed:

- Capacitive touch screen (e.g., TTP223 touch sensor or a more advanced touch screen module)
- Arduino board (e.g., Arduino Uno)
- Jumper wires

Using a Capacitive Touch Sensor (TTP223):

The **TTP223** is a simple capacitive touch sensor module that can be used to detect a touch. It is commonly used for creating touch-based on/off switches in Arduino projects.

Wiring the TTP223:

1. Connect the **VCC** pin to **5V** on the Arduino.
2. Connect the **GND** pin to **GND** on the Arduino.
3. Connect the **SIG** pin to a digital input pin on the Arduino (e.g., pin 7).

Code for Capacitive Touch Detection:

cpp

```cpp
int touchPin = 7;   // Pin connected to TTP223
touch sensor
int ledPin = 13;    // Pin connected to the LED

void setup() {
  pinMode(touchPin, INPUT);   // Set touch pin as
input
  pinMode(ledPin, OUTPUT);     // Set LED pin as
output
  Serial.begin(9600);              // Start serial
communication
}

void loop() {
  int touchState = digitalRead(touchPin);    //
Read touch sensor state

  if (touchState == HIGH) {
    Serial.println("Touch Detected!");
```

113

```
   digitalWrite(ledPin, HIGH);   // Turn on LED
 } else {
   digitalWrite(ledPin, LOW);    // Turn off LED
 }

  delay(100);     // Delay to avoid too many
readings
}
```

Explanation:

- The code reads the state of the touch sensor. When a touch is detected (i.e., the sensor reads HIGH), the LED is turned on, and a message is printed to the serial monitor.

Practical Project: Building a Keypad-Controlled Door Lock

In this practical project, we'll combine the matrix keypad and an electronic lock to create a simple door lock system. The system will allow access only if the correct password is entered on the keypad. The lock will be controlled by a servo motor.

Materials Needed:

- 4x4 Matrix Keypad
- Arduino board (e.g., Arduino Uno)
- Servo motor (e.g., SG90)
- Jumper wires
- Breadboard (optional)

Wiring the Components:

1. **Keypad**: Connect the keypad to 8 digital pins on the Arduino (as we did in the previous section).
2. **Servo**: Connect the **control pin** of the servo to a PWM-capable pin on Arduino (e.g., pin 9).
   o Connect the **VCC** pin to 5V and the **GND** pin to GND.

Code for Keypad-Controlled Door Lock:

cpp

```cpp
#include <Keypad.h>
#include <Servo.h>

// Keypad configuration
const byte ROW_NUM = 4;
const byte COLUMN_NUM = 4;
char keys[ROW_NUM][COLUMN_NUM] = {
  {'1','2','3','A'},
  {'4','5','6','B'},
```

```
  {'7','8','9','C'},
  {'*','0','#','D'}
};
byte pin_rows[ROW_NUM] = {9, 8, 7, 6};  // Connect
to row pinouts
byte pin_column[COLUMN_NUM] = {5, 4, 3, 2};  //
Connect to column pinouts

Keypad    keypad    =    Keypad(makeKeymap(keys),
pin_rows, pin_column, ROW_NUM, COLUMN_NUM);

// Servo setup
Servo myServo;
int doorPin = 9;  // Servo control pin
String correctPassword = "123A";   // Set the
correct password

void setup() {
  myServo.attach(doorPin);   // Attach servo to
pin 9
  myServo.write(0);   // Initial position of the
door (locked)

  Serial.begin(9600);
}

void loop() {
  String enteredPassword = "";   // To store
entered password
```

```
  char key = keypad.getKey();  // Get the pressed
key

  if (key) {
    enteredPassword += key;  // Append the key to
the password
    Serial.print(key);   // Display the entered
key

    if       (enteredPassword.length()       >=
correctPassword.length()) {
      if (enteredPassword == correctPassword) {
        Serial.println("\nPassword     Correct!
Unlocking door...");
        myServo.write(90);   // Unlock the door
(servo to 90 degrees)
        delay(5000);    // Wait for 5 seconds
(simulating the door being unlocked)
        myServo.write(0);  // Lock the door again
        enteredPassword = "";   // Clear the
password
      } else {
        Serial.println("\nIncorrect password!");
        enteredPassword = "";   // Reset the
entered password if wrong
      }
    }
  }
}
```

Explanation:

- The code checks for key presses on the keypad and stores the entered characters in a string.
- When the correct password (in this case, 123A) is entered, the servo motor turns 90 degrees to simulate unlocking the door.
- After 5 seconds, the servo motor returns to its initial position (locked), and the system is ready for the next input.

Conclusion

In this chapter, you learned how to work with **matrix keypads** and **capacitive touch screens** to create interactive input systems. We discussed how to interface with matrix keypads, which are great for entering numerical data or passwords, and capacitive touch sensors, which offer a modern and intuitive way to detect user interaction. You also built a practical project—a **keypad-controlled door lock**—to apply these input techniques in a real-world scenario. These advanced input methods can significantly enhance the functionality of your Arduino projects, making them more interactive and user-friendly. Keep experimenting and building more complex input-based projects!

CHAPTER 12

ARDUINO AND INTERNET OF THINGS (IOT)

In this chapter, we'll explore the **Internet of Things (IoT)** and how Arduino can be integrated into IoT systems. The IoT involves connecting everyday physical objects to the internet, allowing them to send and receive data, interact with other devices, or be controlled remotely. We'll discuss the fundamental principles of IoT, the tools you need to connect Arduino to the internet, and build a practical project where Arduino sends data to the cloud.

Introduction to IoT and Its Applications

The **Internet of Things (IoT)** is a network of physical devices, vehicles, appliances, and other objects embedded with sensors, software, and other technologies to collect and exchange data. These devices can communicate over the internet, enabling automation, monitoring, and control from remote locations.

Applications of IoT:

- **Smart Homes**: Automating household devices like lights, thermostats, and security systems, allowing control through smartphones or voice assistants.
- **Health Monitoring**: Wearable devices that track health metrics (e.g., heart rate, steps) and send data to the cloud for analysis.
- **Industrial IoT**: Monitoring industrial machines, optimizing production lines, and detecting maintenance needs before they lead to breakdowns.
- **Agriculture**: IoT sensors can monitor soil moisture, temperature, and other factors to automate irrigation systems.

In an IoT system, the **sensors** collect data, the **Arduino** processes it, and the **internet** allows that data to be sent to remote servers or cloud platforms where it can be analyzed or accessed by other devices.

Connecting Arduino to the Internet Using Ethernet/Wi-Fi Shields

To integrate Arduino with the IoT, you need a way to connect the board to the internet. Arduino doesn't have built-in networking capabilities, but you can use shields to enable internet connectivity.

Ethernet Shield:

The **Ethernet Shield** allows Arduino to connect to the internet through a wired Ethernet connection. The Ethernet Shield plugs into the Arduino and provides an RJ45 port for connecting to your router.

Wi-Fi Shield:

The **Wi-Fi Shield** enables wireless internet connectivity. It connects to a Wi-Fi network and allows Arduino to communicate over the internet without the need for wires. This is ideal for projects where mobility or installation flexibility is important.

ESP8266 (Wi-Fi Module):

Another popular option for wireless IoT projects is the **ESP8266** module. This low-cost Wi-Fi module can be used to add Wi-Fi capabilities to Arduino. It connects to the internet and can send data to web servers, cloud platforms, or receive commands from a web interface.

Materials Needed:

- Arduino board (e.g., Arduino Uno)
- Ethernet shield or ESP8266 Wi-Fi module
- Jumper wires
- Breadboard (optional)

Connecting Arduino to the Internet with Ethernet Shield

Let's start by exploring how to connect Arduino to the internet using the **Ethernet Shield**. The following example demonstrates how to connect your Arduino to a web server and send data.

Wiring the Ethernet Shield:

1. Connect the **Ethernet Shield** to the Arduino board.
2. Plug the Ethernet cable into the shield and connect it to your router.

Code to Send Data to a Web Server:

To send data to the internet, we'll use the **Ethernet** library. This library provides functions to establish a network connection and send data.

cpp

```cpp
#include <SPI.h>
#include <Ethernet.h>

// Define the MAC address and IP address
byte mac[] = { 0xDE, 0xAD, 0xBE, 0xEF, 0xFE, 0xED
};
IPAddress ip(192, 168, 1, 177);    // Set the
Arduino's static IP address

EthernetClient client;

void setup() {
  Serial.begin(9600);         //   Start   serial
communication
  Ethernet.begin(mac, ip);    // Initialize the
Ethernet shield with a static IP
  delay(1000);

  if (client.connect("example.com", 80)) {   //
Connect to a web server (replace with actual
IP/domain)
    Serial.println("Connected to server");
    client.print("GET     /path/to/api?data=1234
HTTP/1.1\n");  // Send data to the server
    client.println("Host: example.com");
    client.println("Connection: close\n");
  } else {
```

```
    Serial.println("Connection failed");
  }
}


void loop() {
  if (client.available()) {
    char c = client.read();   // Read incoming
data
    Serial.print(c);  // Print data to the serial
monitor
  }

  if (!client.connected()) {
    Serial.println("Closing connection");
    client.stop();  // Close the connection
    delay(5000);   // Wait for 5 seconds before
trying again
  }
}
```

Explanation:

- In the setup(), the Ethernet shield is initialized with a static IP address (you can also use Ethernet.begin(mac) for dynamic IP addressing).
- The code sends an HTTP GET request to a web server (example.com in this case) with some data in the query string.

125

- The server responds, and the response is printed to the serial monitor.

You can replace `"example.com"` with the IP address or domain name of your own server or cloud endpoint to send data to it.

Connecting Arduino to the Internet with ESP8266

If you're using the **ESP8266** module for Wi-Fi, you can connect Arduino to the internet wirelessly. The ESP8266 communicates with Arduino through **SoftwareSerial** (for communication on different pins).

Wiring the ESP8266:

1. Connect the **TX** pin of the ESP8266 to the **RX** pin (pin 2) of Arduino.
2. Connect the **RX** pin of the ESP8266 to the **TX** pin (pin 3) of Arduino.
3. Connect **VCC** and **CH_PD** to 3.3V on the Arduino.
4. Connect **GND** to GND on Arduino.

Code to Connect to Wi-Fi and Send Data to the Cloud:

```cpp
#include <SoftwareSerial.h>
#include <ESP8266WiFi.h>

SoftwareSerial espSerial(2, 3);  // RX, TX pins
for ESP8266
const char* ssid = "your_network_name";  // Wi-
Fi network name
const char* password = "your_password";  // Wi-
Fi password

WiFiClient client;

void setup() {
  Serial.begin(9600);
  espSerial.begin(115200);            //       Start
communication with ESP8266

  WiFi.begin(ssid, password);  // Connect to Wi-
Fi
  while (WiFi.status() != WL_CONNECTED) {
    delay(1000);
    Serial.print(".");
  }
  Serial.println("Connected to Wi-Fi");

  if (client.connect("example.com", 80)) {  //
Connect to a cloud server
```

```
    client.print("GET          /data?value=5678
HTTP/1.1\n");   // Send data to the server
    client.println("Host: example.com");
    client.println("Connection: close\n");
  } else {
    Serial.println("Connection failed");
  }
}


void loop() {
  if (client.available()) {
    char c = client.read();   // Read incoming
data from the server
    Serial.print(c);   // Print the response to
the serial monitor
  }

  if (!client.connected()) {
    Serial.println("Closing connection");
    client.stop();   // Close the connection
    delay(5000);   // Wait before reconnecting
  }
}
```

Explanation:

- The code connects to a Wi-Fi network using the **WiFi.begin()** function.

- It then sends a request to a web server (or cloud platform) to send some data (in this case, `value=5678`).
- The response from the server is printed to the serial monitor.

You can replace `"example.com"` with the IP address or domain of a cloud platform (such as **ThingSpeak** or **Adafruit IO**) to send data.

Practical Project: Sending Data to the Cloud

Now that you know how to connect Arduino to the internet, let's build a practical IoT project that sends data to the cloud. We will use **ThingSpeak**, a cloud platform that allows you to visualize and analyze IoT data. You will send data from a sensor (e.g., a temperature sensor) to ThingSpeak, where you can monitor it remotely.

Materials Needed:

- Arduino board (e.g., Arduino Uno)
- Ethernet shield or ESP8266 Wi-Fi module
- DHT11 or DHT22 temperature and humidity sensor
- Jumper wires
- Breadboard (optional)

Steps:

1. Set up a **ThingSpeak** account and create a channel.
2. Obtain your **Write API Key** from the ThingSpeak channel.
3. Connect your sensor (e.g., DHT11) to Arduino.

Code to Send Data to ThingSpeak:

cpp

```cpp
#include <SPI.h>
#include <Ethernet.h>
#include <DHT.h>

DHT dht(2, DHT11);  // Pin 2 for DHT11 sensor

// Ethernet settings
byte mac[] = { 0xDE, 0xAD, 0xBE, 0xEF, 0xFE, 0xED
};
IPAddress ip(192, 168, 1, 177);
EthernetClient client;

char server[] = "api.thingspeak.com";
String apiKey = "YOUR_WRITE_API_KEY";  // Replace
with your ThingSpeak API key

void setup() {
  Serial.begin(9600);
```

```
  Ethernet.begin(mac, ip);
  dht.begin();  // Start the DHT sensor
  delay(1000);
}


void loop() {
  float temperature = dht.readTemperature();  //
Read temperature
  float humidity = dht.readHumidity();  // Read
humidity

  if (client.connect(server, 80)) {
    // Send data to ThingSpeak
    client.print("GET /update?key=");
    client.print(apiKey);
    client.print("&field1=");
    client.print(temperature);
    client.print("&field2=");
    client.print(humidity);
    client.println(" HTTP/1.1");
    client.println("Host: api.thingspeak.com");
    client.println("Connection: close");
    client.println();
  }

  delay(20000);  // Wait for 20 seconds before
sending next data
}
```

Explanation:

- The DHT sensor is used to measure temperature and humidity.
- The Arduino connects to ThingSpeak using the **Ethernet** library (or **Wi-Fi** if using the ESP8266).
- The sensor data is sent to ThingSpeak every 20 seconds.

You can view the data on your ThingSpeak dashboard in real-time.

Conclusion

In this chapter, you learned how to integrate Arduino with the **Internet of Things (IoT)** by connecting it to the internet using Ethernet or Wi-Fi shields. We explored how to send data to the cloud using platforms like ThingSpeak and worked on practical projects like sending sensor data to the cloud. With IoT, you can now create remote monitoring systems, smart devices, and data-logging applications that are connected to the internet. This opens up endless possibilities for creating intelligent systems that can be controlled or monitored remotely. Keep experimenting with IoT and expand your projects!

CHAPTER 13

ARDUINO AND HOME AUTOMATION

In this chapter, we'll explore how to use Arduino in **home automation**, a rapidly growing field that enables you to control home devices such as lights, thermostats, security systems, and appliances remotely. We'll discuss the basic concepts of home automation, how to build smart devices with Arduino, and create a practical project—a smart light system that can be controlled via a mobile app.

Basic Concepts of Home Automation

Home automation refers to the use of technology to control and automate various household functions, typically through an internet-connected device or smartphone. This can include controlling lights, locks, heating, cooling systems, and other electronic devices automatically or remotely. The goal is to improve convenience, efficiency, and security within the home.

Key Components of Home Automation:

1. **Smart Devices**: These are the devices in your home that can be controlled automatically or remotely. Examples include smart bulbs, thermostats, and smart locks.
2. **Control Interface**: This can be a smartphone, tablet, or computer that interacts with the smart devices. The user sends commands to the devices via apps or web interfaces.
3. **Connectivity**: Smart devices need to communicate with each other and the control interface. This is typically done through **Wi-Fi**, **Bluetooth**, **Zigbee**, or **Z-Wave**.
4. **Sensors and Actuators**: Sensors (e.g., temperature sensors, motion detectors) collect data, while actuators (e.g., motors, lights) perform actions based on that data. Arduino can serve as the central controller to interpret sensor data and control actuators.

Benefits of Home Automation:

- **Convenience**: Control devices remotely via your phone or automation systems.
- **Energy Efficiency**: Automate systems like lighting and heating to minimize energy waste.
- **Security**: Monitor and control locks, security cameras, and alarms remotely.

Building Smart Devices with Arduino

Arduino is an excellent platform for building home automation systems because it allows for easy integration with sensors, actuators, and communication modules. By combining Arduino with modules such as **Wi-Fi shields**, **Bluetooth modules**, and **relays**, you can control home devices with ease.

Smart Devices You Can Build with Arduino:

- **Smart Lights**: Control lighting remotely or automatically based on conditions (e.g., time of day or motion detection).
- **Smart Thermostats**: Automatically adjust temperature based on user preferences or sensor data.
- **Smart Security Systems**: Monitor doors, windows, and other entry points for motion or door status and alert the user.
- **Smart Appliances**: Automate the operation of devices like coffee makers, fans, and even curtains.

Practical Project: Creating a Smart Light System Controlled via a Mobile App

In this project, we will create a simple smart light system that can be turned on or off via a mobile app. We'll use **Arduino** with a **Wi-Fi module (ESP8266)**, and a smartphone app to control the light remotely. This project will help you understand how to interface Arduino with home automation systems and control devices wirelessly.

Materials Needed:

- Arduino board (e.g., Arduino Uno)
- ESP8266 Wi-Fi module
- Relay module (to control the light)
- Lamp (or any other device that can be controlled via a relay)
- Jumper wires
- Breadboard (optional)
- Smartphone with a mobile app (e.g., Blynk)

Wiring the Components:

1. **ESP8266 Module**:
   - Connect the **TX** and **RX** pins of the ESP8266 to **RX** and **TX** pins of Arduino, respectively.

- o Connect **VCC** to 3.3V (note: the ESP8266 operates on 3.3V, not 5V).
- o Connect **GND** to GND on Arduino.

2. **Relay Module**:
   - o Connect the **VCC** and **GND** pins of the relay to **5V** and **GND** on Arduino.
   - o Connect the **IN** pin of the relay to a digital output pin on Arduino (e.g., pin 7).

3. **Lamp**:
   - o Connect the lamp to the relay's **NO (Normally Open)** and **COM (Common)** pins. When the relay is triggered, the circuit will close, turning on the lamp.

Creating the Mobile App with Blynk

Blynk is a popular mobile app platform that allows you to create custom interfaces to control your Arduino projects. It offers a drag-and-drop interface for creating buttons, sliders, and other controls that communicate with Arduino via the internet.

Steps to Create a Mobile App:

1. **Download the Blynk App**:

o   Install the Blynk app on your smartphone (available for iOS and Android).

2. **Create a New Project**:

    o   Open the app and create a new project.

    o   Choose the **ESP8266** as your device type.

    o   Select the **Wi-Fi** connection type.

    o   You will receive a **token** that you'll use in your Arduino code for communication with the app.

3. **Add a Button to Control the Light**:

    o   In the Blynk app, add a **Button Widget** to your project. This button will control the state of the light.

    o   Set the button to switch between **ON/OFF** states.

4. **Note the Auth Token**:

    o   The app will generate a **Auth Token** that you will need to use in the Arduino code to allow communication between the app and the Arduino.

Arduino Code for Controlling the Light:

Now that the app is set up, let's move on to the Arduino code. We'll use the **Blynk** library to communicate with the app and control the relay.

Arduino Code:

cpp

```cpp
#include <ESP8266WiFi.h>
#include <BlynkSimpleEsp8266.h>

// Your Wi-Fi credentials and Blynk Auth Token
char auth[] = "Your_Blynk_Auth_Token";    // Replace with your Blynk Auth Token
char ssid[] = "Your_WiFi_SSID";          // Replace with your Wi-Fi SSID
char pass[] = "Your_WiFi_Password";      // Replace with your Wi-Fi Password

int relayPin = 7;   // Pin connected to relay module

void setup() {
  Serial.begin(9600);
  Blynk.begin(auth, ssid, pass);   // Connect to Blynk server

  pinMode(relayPin, OUTPUT);   // Set relay pin as output
  digitalWrite(relayPin, LOW);   // Initially turn off the relay (light off)
}

void loop() {
  Blynk.run();   // Run the Blynk app
```

```
}


// This function will be called when the button
in the Blynk app is pressed
BLYNK_WRITE(V1) {  // V1 is the virtual pin linked
to the button in the app
  int pinValue = param.asInt();  // Get the value
of the button (0 or 1)
  if (pinValue == 1) {
    digitalWrite(relayPin, HIGH);   // Turn the
light ON
  } else {
    digitalWrite(relayPin, LOW);    // Turn the
light OFF
  }
}
```

Explanation:

- **Wi-Fi Setup**: The Arduino connects to your Wi-Fi network using the `ESP8266` module. It uses the provided SSID and password.

- **Blynk Communication**: The `Blynk.begin()` function connects to the Blynk server using your **Auth Token**.

- **Relay Control**: When the button in the Blynk app is pressed, it sends a signal to the Arduino. The Arduino reads this signal and controls the relay, which turns the light on or off.

Testing the System

1. Upload the code to the Arduino.
2. Open the **Blynk app** and press the button on the mobile app.
3. The relay should activate, turning the light on or off, depending on the button state.

Conclusion

In this chapter, you learned how to use Arduino for **home automation** by building a smart light system. We discussed the key concepts of home automation and how to use **Wi-Fi modules** like the **ESP8266** to connect Arduino to the internet. You also created a mobile app with **Blynk** to control a light system remotely. Home automation projects like this one open up endless possibilities for creating smarter, more efficient homes. Experiment with other devices like fans, thermostats, or security systems to expand your smart home!

CHAPTER 14

WIRELESS COMMUNICATION: RF AND IR MODULES

In this chapter, we will explore two common wireless communication methods used in Arduino projects: **Radio Frequency (RF)** communication and **Infrared (IR)** communication. Both of these technologies allow Arduino to wirelessly communicate with other devices, making them ideal for remote control systems and various wireless applications. We will also build a practical project: a **remote-controlled car** using RF modules.

Basics of RF Communication and IR Modules

RF Communication

Radio Frequency (RF) communication uses electromagnetic waves to transmit data over a distance. RF modules typically operate on specific frequencies, such as **433 MHz** or **315 MHz**, and can be used for both short-range and long-range wireless communication. RF modules are widely used in remote control systems, wireless sensors, and home automation systems.

- **RF Transmitter and Receiver Modules**: These are paired modules where the **transmitter** sends data, and the **receiver** receives the data. They are usually used in simple systems that require wireless communication between two devices.
- **Advantages**: RF communication can work through obstacles, has a longer range compared to infrared (IR), and can be used in a wide variety of applications.
- **Limitations**: RF modules tend to be more prone to interference, and their communication range can be limited by environmental factors.

IR Communication

Infrared (IR) communication uses light in the infrared spectrum to transmit data. Unlike RF, IR communication requires **line-of-sight** between the transmitter and receiver. IR modules are commonly used in devices like remote controls, where the user points the remote control at the device to send commands.

- **IR Transmitter and Receiver Modules**: The **transmitter** emits infrared light, and the **receiver** detects the light. The data is encoded in the IR light and decoded by the receiver.

- **Advantages**: IR communication is simple, inexpensive, and low power. It is widely used in consumer electronics (e.g., TV remotes).

- **Limitations**: IR communication requires direct line-of-sight and is limited by the range of the infrared light.

Practical Uses in Remote Control Systems

Both **RF** and **IR** modules are commonly used in remote control systems for devices like robots, cars, home appliances, and other electronic systems. Here's how they are used:

RF in Remote Control Systems:

- **RF Transmitter and Receiver** modules can be used in a wireless remote control system to send commands from a remote to a device.

- For example, in a **remote-controlled car**, the RF transmitter sends signals to the RF receiver on the car, which then performs actions such as moving forward, backward, or turning based on the signals received.

IR in Remote Control Systems:

- **IR remote controls** are widely used for controlling TVs, fans, air conditioners, and other appliances. The **IR transmitter** sends a modulated infrared light signal that is decoded by the **IR receiver** on the device, enabling remote control.

- IR communication can be used in Arduino projects where line-of-sight control is sufficient, such as controlling appliances or robots within the range of an IR sensor.

Practical Project: Remote-Controlled Car with RF

In this project, we will build a simple **remote-controlled car** using **RF communication**. The car will be controlled using an RF transmitter, while the receiver module will be connected to the car to control its movement.

Materials Needed:

- Arduino board (e.g., Arduino Uno)
- 433 MHz RF Transmitter and Receiver Modules
- DC motors with wheels (for the car)
- L298N Motor Driver Module (for controlling the motors)
- Jumper wires

- Battery pack (for powering the car)
- Chassis (can be made from plastic or a pre-built robot car kit)
- Breadboard (optional)
- Push buttons or joystick for controlling the RF transmitter

Wiring the Components:

Transmitter Side (Remote Control):

1. **RF Transmitter**: Connect the **DATA** pin of the transmitter to a digital pin (e.g., pin 12) on the Arduino.
2. **Button/Joystick**: Connect the push buttons or joystick to the Arduino to control the forward, backward, left, and right movements.
   - For example, use **digital pins** for the buttons (e.g., pin 2 for forward, pin 3 for backward, pin 4 for left, and pin 5 for right).

Receiver Side (Car):

1. **RF Receiver**: Connect the **DATA** pin of the receiver to a digital pin (e.g., pin 8) on the Arduino.
2. **Motor Driver (L298N)**: Connect the L298N motor driver to the motors and the Arduino. The motor driver will control the movement of the motors based on the signals received from the RF receiver.

- o Connect the **IN1**, **IN2**, **IN3**, and **IN4** pins of the motor driver to the Arduino digital pins (e.g., pins 9, 10, 11, 12).
- o Connect the motors to the **M1** and **M2** pins of the L298N.

Code for Transmitter (Remote Control):

The transmitter will send signals based on the button or joystick inputs. When a button is pressed, the corresponding command will be sent to the receiver.

cpp

```
#include <VirtualWire.h>

int forwardButton = 2;   // Button for moving
forward
int backwardButton = 3;  // Button for moving
backward
int leftButton = 4;      // Button for turning
left
int rightButton = 5;     // Button for turning
right

void setup() {
```

```
  Serial.begin(9600);          //    Start    serial
communication
  vw_setup(2000);        // Set the data rate to
2000 bits per second
  vw_set_tx_pin(12);    // Set the transmitter pin
  pinMode(forwardButton, INPUT);
  pinMode(backwardButton, INPUT);
  pinMode(leftButton, INPUT);
  pinMode(rightButton, INPUT);
}


void loop() {
  if (digitalRead(forwardButton) == HIGH) {
    const char *msg = "FORWARD";
    vw_send((uint8_t *)msg, strlen(msg));
    vw_wait_tx();   // Wait until the message is
sent
  }
  if (digitalRead(backwardButton) == HIGH) {
    const char *msg = "BACKWARD";
    vw_send((uint8_t *)msg, strlen(msg));
    vw_wait_tx();
  }
  if (digitalRead(leftButton) == HIGH) {
    const char *msg = "LEFT";
    vw_send((uint8_t *)msg, strlen(msg));
    vw_wait_tx();
  }
  if (digitalRead(rightButton) == HIGH) {
```

```cpp
    const char *msg = "RIGHT";
    vw_send((uint8_t *)msg, strlen(msg));
    vw_wait_tx();
  }
}
```

Code for Receiver (Car):

The receiver will read the signals sent by the transmitter and control the motors accordingly.

cpp

```cpp
#include <VirtualWire.h>

int motorPin1 = 9;   // Motor control pins
int motorPin2 = 10;
int motorPin3 = 11;
int motorPin4 = 12;

void setup() {
  Serial.begin(9600);        //    Start    serial
communication
  vw_setup(2000);        // Set the data rate to
2000 bits per second
  vw_set_rx_pin(8);    // Set the receiver pin
  vw_rx_start();          // Start the receiver
  pinMode(motorPin1, OUTPUT);
```

```
  pinMode(motorPin2, OUTPUT);
  pinMode(motorPin3, OUTPUT);
  pinMode(motorPin4, OUTPUT);
}

void loop() {
  uint8_t message[4];
  uint8_t messageLength = 4;

  if (vw_get_message(message, &messageLength)) {
    String msg = String((char *)message);
    Serial.println(msg);  // Print the received
message

    if (msg == "FORWARD") {
      // Move forward
      digitalWrite(motorPin1, HIGH);
      digitalWrite(motorPin2, LOW);
      digitalWrite(motorPin3, HIGH);
      digitalWrite(motorPin4, LOW);
    } else if (msg == "BACKWARD") {
      // Move backward
      digitalWrite(motorPin1, LOW);
      digitalWrite(motorPin2, HIGH);
      digitalWrite(motorPin3, LOW);
      digitalWrite(motorPin4, HIGH);
    } else if (msg == "LEFT") {
      // Turn left
      digitalWrite(motorPin1, LOW);
```

```
      digitalWrite(motorPin2, HIGH);
      digitalWrite(motorPin3, HIGH);
      digitalWrite(motorPin4, LOW);
    } else if (msg == "RIGHT") {
      // Turn right
      digitalWrite(motorPin1, HIGH);
      digitalWrite(motorPin2, LOW);
      digitalWrite(motorPin3, LOW);
      digitalWrite(motorPin4, HIGH);
    }
  }
}
```

Explanation:

- The **transmitter** sends a command when a button is pressed (e.g., "FORWARD", "BACKWARD", "LEFT", or "RIGHT").
- The **receiver** receives the command and moves the car in the corresponding direction by controlling the motor driver.

Conclusion

In this chapter, you learned how to use **RF communication** with Arduino for building a **remote-controlled car**. We covered the basics of **RF and IR communication**, how they are used in remote control systems, and created a practical project where RF signals were used to control a car. This setup can be extended for other IoT applications, such as smart home devices, security systems, or robotic systems. The possibilities are endless when it comes to wireless communication with Arduino!

CHAPTER 15

DATA LOGGING WITH ARDUINO

In this chapter, we'll explore how to use **Arduino** for **data logging** applications. Data logging is the process of recording data over time, which is useful for monitoring and analyzing trends, performing experiments, or tracking conditions over long periods. We'll focus on using **SD cards** to store sensor data and build a practical project where temperature and humidity readings are logged over time.

Introduction to Data Logging Systems

Data logging systems are used to collect and store data from various sources over a period of time. These systems are commonly used in applications such as:

- **Environmental monitoring**: Collecting data on temperature, humidity, air quality, etc.
- **Scientific experiments**: Logging sensor data for research purposes.
- **Industrial monitoring**: Tracking equipment performance, system status, or operational parameters.

- **Home automation**: Monitoring temperature, humidity, or energy usage in a smart home.

The key component of a data logging system is the **data storage medium**, where sensor data is saved for future analysis. One of the most commonly used storage mediums in Arduino projects is the **SD card**, which allows large amounts of data to be stored and easily retrieved.

Using SD Cards to Store Sensor Data

An **SD card** (Secure Digital card) is a portable, non-volatile memory card that can store large amounts of data. The Arduino can interface with an SD card using an **SD card module** or shield, allowing it to read and write data.

Components Needed for Data Logging:

- **Arduino board** (e.g., Arduino Uno)
- **SD card module** or **SD card shield**
- **MicroSD card** (formatted as FAT16 or FAT32)
- **Temperature and humidity sensor** (e.g., DHT11 or DHT22)
- **Jumper wires**
- **Breadboard** (optional)

Wiring the Components:

1. **SD Card Module**:
   - **VCC** pin to **5V** on the Arduino
   - **GND** pin to **GND** on the Arduino
   - **MISO** pin to pin **12** on the Arduino
   - **MOSI** pin to pin **11** on the Arduino
   - **SCK** pin to pin **13** on the Arduino
   - **CS** pin to pin **4** on the Arduino (can be changed in the code)

2. **DHT11 Sensor**:
   - **VCC** pin to **5V** on the Arduino
   - **GND** pin to **GND** on the Arduino
   - **DATA** pin to **pin 2** on the Arduino (can be changed in the code)

Practical Project: Data Logging for Temperature and Humidity

In this practical project, we will log the temperature and humidity readings from a **DHT11 sensor** and store the data on an **SD card**. This project will help you understand how to read sensor data and write it to a file on the SD card.

Code for Data Logging:

First, you'll need to install the necessary libraries for the **DHT11 sensor** and the **SD card module**. You can install these libraries through the **Arduino Library Manager**.

1. **DHT Sensor Library**: Search for the **DHT sensor library** by Adafruit and install it.
2. **SD Card Library**: This library is built into the Arduino IDE, so no installation is required.

Here's the code to read temperature and humidity from the DHT11 sensor and log the data to the SD card.

cpp

```
#include <SPI.h>
#include <SD.h>
#include <DHT.h>

#define DHTPIN 2          // Pin where the DHT11
is connected
#define DHTTYPE DHT11     // Define the sensor
type (DHT11 or DHT22)

DHT dht(DHTPIN, DHTTYPE); // Create an instance
of the DHT sensor
File dataFile;
```

```
const int chipSelect = 4;   // SD card chip select
pin

void setup() {
  Serial.begin(9600);
  dht.begin();  // Initialize the DHT sensor

  // Initialize SD card
  if (!SD.begin(chipSelect)) {
    Serial.println("Initialization failed!");
    return;
  }
  Serial.println("Initialization done.");

  // Open the file on the SD card for writing
(create a new file if it doesn't exist)
  dataFile = SD.open("log.txt", FILE_WRITE);

  if (dataFile) {
    Serial.println("Logging data...");
    dataFile.println("Temperature (C), Humidity
(%)");  // Log the headers
    dataFile.close();   // Close the file after
writing headers
  } else {
    Serial.println("Error opening log.txt");
  }
}
```

```
void loop() {
  // Read humidity and temperature
  float humidity = dht.readHumidity();
  float temperature = dht.readTemperature();

  // Check if reading failed
  if (isnan(humidity) || isnan(temperature)) {
    Serial.println("Failed  to  read  from  DHT
sensor!");
    return;
  }

  // Print the data to the serial monitor
  Serial.print("Temperature: ");
  Serial.print(temperature);
  Serial.print(" °C ");
  Serial.print("Humidity: ");
  Serial.print(humidity);
  Serial.println(" %");

  // Open the file on the SD card for appending
  dataFile = SD.open("log.txt", FILE_WRITE);

  if (dataFile) {
    // Write the temperature and humidity data to
the file
    dataFile.print(temperature);
    dataFile.print(", ");
    dataFile.println(humidity);
```

```
    dataFile.close();    // Close the file after
writing
  } else {
    Serial.println("Error opening log.txt");
  }


  delay(2000);    // Wait for 2 seconds before
taking another reading
}
```

Explanation:

- The code reads the temperature and humidity values from the **DHT11 sensor** every 2 seconds.
- The **SD card** is initialized using the `SD.begin()` function, and a new file called `log.txt` is created (or opened if it already exists).
- The sensor data is logged to the file in CSV format (e.g., "25.3, 60.2") and is saved to the SD card.
- The file is closed after every write operation to ensure that data is saved properly.
- You can view the logged data by removing the SD card and reading the file on a computer or by printing it to the serial monitor.

Testing the Data Logging System

1. Upload the code to the Arduino board.
2. Open the **Serial Monitor** to see the temperature and humidity readings being printed.
3. After a few readings, remove the **microSD card** from the module and insert it into your computer.
4. Open the `log.txt` file on your computer to view the logged data, which should look something like this:

scss

```
Temperature (C), Humidity (%)
25.3, 60.2
25.5, 61.0
25.4, 60.5
```

You can now use this data for further analysis or to monitor environmental conditions over time.

Conclusion

In this chapter, you learned how to use **Arduino** for **data logging** applications, particularly with the **SD card module**. We explored how to store sensor data (temperature and humidity readings) on an SD card and reviewed the steps to read and write data to a file. Data logging is an essential component for many Arduino projects, especially for applications that require long-term monitoring and analysis. You can extend this project to log other sensor data, such as light levels, air quality, or pressure, and use it for monitoring or reporting purposes.

CHAPTER 16

WORKING WITH SERVOS AND ROBOTICS

In this chapter, we will explore **servos** and their applications in **robotics**. Servos are widely used in robotics for precise control of movement, making them an essential component for building robots and automation systems. We will discuss how servos work, how to control multiple servos, and then create a practical project—a simple robotic arm using Arduino and servos.

Understanding Servos and Their Applications in Robotics

A **servo motor** is a type of motor that allows precise control of angular position, speed, and acceleration. It consists of a small DC motor, a set of gears, and a control circuit. The main feature of a servo is its ability to rotate to a specific position based on the input control signal. Servos are widely used in applications where controlled movement is required, such as robotics, camera pans, robotic arms, and more.

How Servos Work

Servos are controlled by sending **Pulse Width Modulation (PWM)** signals. The width of the pulse determines the angle at which the servo's arm will move. The basic components of a servo are:

- **Motor**: Provides the rotational force.
- **Feedback mechanism**: Allows the servo to determine its current position.
- **Control circuit**: Receives the PWM signal and adjusts the motor's rotation to reach the desired position.

Applications of Servos in Robotics

- **Robotic Arms**: Servos are used to move the joints of robotic arms with high precision.
- **Wheeled Robots**: Servos can control the steering or movement of robots.
- **Pan-and-Tilt Systems**: Servos are often used in camera or sensor systems that need to change orientation.

Controlling Multiple Servos for Robot Movements

When building more advanced robots, controlling multiple servos simultaneously is essential for coordinated movements. Arduino makes it easy to control multiple servos, and there are libraries available to simplify the process.

Controlling Multiple Servos:

To control multiple servos, we can use the **Servo** library in Arduino, which simplifies controlling the angle of servos by sending the appropriate PWM signal.

Materials Needed:

- Arduino board (e.g., Arduino Uno)
- 3x Standard Servos (e.g., SG90)
- Jumper wires
- Power supply (for powering the servos)
- Breadboard (optional)
- Servo mounting hardware (optional)

Wiring the Servos:

1. **Connect the power**: Servos usually operate at 5V, so connect the **VCC** pins of the servos to the **5V** pin on the Arduino.
2. **Connect the ground**: Connect all **GND** pins from the servos to **GND** on the Arduino.
3. **Control Pins**: Connect the control pins of the servos to three **digital pins** on Arduino (e.g., pins 9, 10, and 11).

Arduino Code to Control Multiple Servos:

Here's a basic example that controls three servos, each moving to different angles.

cpp

```cpp
#include <Servo.h>  // Include the Servo library

// Create Servo objects
Servo servo1;
Servo servo2;
Servo servo3;

void setup() {
  // Attach servos to pins
  servo1.attach(9);  // Servo 1 on pin 9
  servo2.attach(10); // Servo 2 on pin 10
  servo3.attach(11); // Servo 3 on pin 11
}
```

```
void loop() {
  // Move the servos to different angles
  servo1.write(0);   // Move servo 1 to 0 degrees
  servo2.write(90);   // Move servo 2 to 90
degrees
  servo3.write(180);  // Move servo 3 to 180
degrees

  delay(1000);  // Wait for 1 second

  servo1.write(90);   // Move servo 1 to 90
degrees
  servo2.write(180);  // Move servo 2 to 180
degrees
  servo3.write(0);   // Move servo 3 to 0 degrees

  delay(1000);  // Wait for 1 second
}
```

Explanation:

- The **Servo** library is used to control the position of the servos.
- Each servo is assigned to a digital pin (9, 10, and 11).
- The `write()` function is used to set the angle of each servo (ranging from 0° to 180°).
- The servos move to different positions in a loop, with delays to make the movement visible.

166

Practical Project: Building a Simple Robotic Arm

Now that we understand how to control multiple servos, let's create a simple **robotic arm** that uses servos to simulate the movement of a human arm. The robotic arm will have 3 degrees of freedom (DOF), controlled by 3 servos: one for the base (rotation), one for the elbow (up and down), and one for the wrist (gripper).

Materials Needed:

- Arduino board (e.g., Arduino Uno)
- 3x Servos (e.g., SG90 or MG90)
- Jumper wires
- Breadboard (optional)
- Power supply for the servos (optional)
- Robotic arm chassis or materials to create one (can be made with plastic or 3D-printed parts)

Wiring the Components:

1. **Servo 1 (Base Rotation)**: Connect to pin 9 on Arduino.
2. **Servo 2 (Elbow Movement)**: Connect to pin 10 on Arduino.

3. **Servo 3 (Wrist/Gripper Movement)**: Connect to pin 11 on Arduino.

4. **Power Supply**: Ensure that the servos have an adequate power source if they are high-power servos (e.g., 6V battery pack).

Assembly of the Robotic Arm:

1. **Base Servo**: Attach the servo to the base of the arm to control rotation (left and right).

2. **Elbow Servo**: Attach the second servo to the middle section of the arm to control the up-and-down movement (like an elbow joint).

3. **Wrist/Gripper Servo**: The third servo will control the gripper, or wrist joint, enabling the arm to open and close.

Code for Robotic Arm Movement:

cpp

```
#include <Servo.h>

// Create Servo objects
Servo baseServo;   // Base rotation
Servo elbowServo; // Elbow movement
Servo wristServo; // Wrist/Gripper movement

void setup() {
```

```
  // Attach the servos to the corresponding pins
  baseServo.attach(9);
  elbowServo.attach(10);
  wristServo.attach(11);
}

void loop() {
  // Move the base (rotation)
  baseServo.write(45);    // Rotate 45 degrees
  delay(1000);
  baseServo.write(135);   // Rotate 135 degrees
  delay(1000);

  // Move the elbow (up and down)
  elbowServo.write(30);   // Move the elbow to 30
degrees
  delay(1000);
  elbowServo.write(90);   // Move the elbow to 90
degrees
  delay(1000);

  // Move the wrist (gripper open and close)
  wristServo.write(0);    // Close the gripper (0
degrees)
  delay(1000);
  wristServo.write(90);   // Open the gripper (90
degrees)
  delay(1000);
}
```

Explanation:

- The **baseServo**, **elbowServo**, and **wristServo** are controlled by their respective digital pins (9, 10, and 11).
- The servos are moved to different angles to simulate the movements of the robotic arm.
- The gripper opens and closes, and the arm rotates and bends by adjusting the angles of the servos.

Conclusion

In this chapter, you learned how to work with **servos** in Arduino and explored their applications in **robotics**. We discussed how to control multiple servos to perform coordinated movements, such as building a **robotic arm** with different degrees of freedom. Servos are essential components in many robotic applications, enabling precise control of movement. With the knowledge you've gained, you can start building more complex robotic systems, like robotic hands, drones, or even mobile robots that can interact with their environment. Keep experimenting and expanding your robotic creations!

CHAPTER 17

BUILDING A SMART SECURITY SYSTEM

In this chapter, we will explore how to build a **smart security system** using **Arduino**. Security systems are used to monitor and protect properties from unauthorized access, theft, or damage. We will discuss the basic components of security systems, such as sensors, cameras, and alarms, and learn how to integrate them with Arduino. We'll also build a practical project: a **motion-activated security system** that triggers an alarm when motion is detected.

Overview of Security Systems and Sensors

A security system is designed to monitor an area and detect any unauthorized activity, such as movement, tampering, or breaches. It typically includes a combination of sensors, cameras, and alarms to secure the area.

Key Components of a Security System:

1. **Cameras**: Surveillance cameras allow real-time video monitoring of the area. They can be connected to a system to send alerts when motion or unusual activity is detected.

2. **Motion Sensors**: These sensors detect movement within a defined area. They are commonly used in security systems to detect intruders. Common types of motion sensors include **PIR (Passive Infrared) sensors**, which detect infrared radiation from the human body.

3. **Alarms**: Alarms alert users when an intruder is detected. These can be audible (sirens) or silent (sending notifications to a mobile app or server).

Common Security System Sensors:

- **PIR Motion Sensors**: Detect infrared radiation from objects in motion. These are commonly used for security purposes to detect human movement.

- **Magnetic Door Sensors**: Detect when a door or window is opened or closed by sensing a magnetic field.

- **Vibration Sensors**: Detect physical movement or vibrations, which can indicate tampering with doors or windows.

- **Cameras**: Allow for visual monitoring of the area. They can be connected to the Arduino for triggering specific actions based on motion or other inputs.

Integrating Cameras, Motion Sensors, and Alarms with Arduino

Arduino provides a great platform for integrating various sensors and components to build a smart security system. Here's how you can integrate some key components:

1. PIR Motion Sensor:

A **PIR sensor** detects the motion of people by measuring infrared radiation. It is widely used in home security systems to monitor movement.

- **How It Works**: The sensor detects the infrared radiation emitted by warm bodies (like humans). When motion is detected, it sends a HIGH signal to the Arduino.

2. Cameras:

While Arduino can't process high-resolution camera data directly, you can interface an Arduino with a simple camera module, like the **OV7670** or use a **Raspberry Pi** for advanced camera functionality. For simple projects, you can trigger a camera to take a snapshot when motion is detected.

- **How It Works**: Cameras can be connected to Arduino through a serial interface, and snapshots can be captured when certain conditions are met, like motion detection.

3. Alarms:

An **alarm** can be triggered by Arduino when the system detects motion or an intrusion. It can be a simple **buzzer** or a **loud siren** connected to an output pin on Arduino.

- **How It Works**: When motion is detected by a sensor, the Arduino sends a signal to an alarm (e.g., turning on a buzzer or flashing lights).

Practical Project: Creating a Motion-Activated Security System

In this practical project, we will build a simple **motion-activated security system** using an **Arduino** board, a **PIR motion sensor**, and a **buzzer** as the alarm. When the PIR sensor detects motion, the system will trigger the buzzer to alert you.

Materials Needed:

- Arduino board (e.g., Arduino Uno)
- PIR Motion Sensor
- Buzzer (or siren)
- Jumper wires
- Breadboard (optional)
- Power supply (for Arduino and components)

Wiring the Components:

1. **PIR Motion Sensor**:
   - Connect the **VCC** pin of the PIR sensor to **5V** on the Arduino.
   - Connect the **GND** pin of the PIR sensor to **GND** on the Arduino.
   - Connect the **OUT** pin of the PIR sensor to **digital pin 7** on the Arduino (this pin will detect motion).

2. **Buzzer**:
   - Connect the **positive (longer)** leg of the buzzer to **digital pin 8** on the Arduino.
   - Connect the **negative (shorter)** leg of the buzzer to **GND** on the Arduino.

Code for Motion-Activated Security System:

This code reads the input from the **PIR sensor** and triggers the **buzzer** when motion is detected.

```cpp
int pirPin = 7;    // Pin connected to the PIR
sensor
int buzzerPin = 8; // Pin connected to the buzzer
int pirState = 0;  // Variable to store the PIR
sensor state

void setup() {
  pinMode(pirPin, INPUT);   // Set PIR sensor pin
as input
  pinMode(buzzerPin, OUTPUT);   // Set buzzer pin
as output
  Serial.begin(9600);        //    Start    serial
communication for debugging
}

void loop() {
  pirState = digitalRead(pirPin);   // Read the
state of the PIR sensor

  if (pirState == HIGH) {   // If motion is
detected
    Serial.println("Motion detected! Activating
alarm...");
```

```
    digitalWrite(buzzerPin, HIGH);     // Turn on
the buzzer
  } else {
    digitalWrite(buzzerPin, LOW);      // Turn off
the buzzer when no motion
  }

  delay(100);  // Wait for a short moment before
checking again
}
```

Explanation:

- The PIR sensor is connected to digital pin 7, and the buzzer is connected to digital pin 8.
- The code checks for motion using `digitalRead()` on the PIR sensor. When motion is detected (i.e., the sensor's output pin goes HIGH), the buzzer is triggered by setting the output pin HIGH, turning on the sound.
- The system remains in this state until no motion is detected, at which point the buzzer is turned off.

Testing the Security System

1. Upload the code to the Arduino.

2. Open the **Serial Monitor** to observe the output. The message "Motion detected! Activating alarm..." will be printed to the serial monitor whenever the PIR sensor detects movement.

3. When the PIR sensor detects motion, the **buzzer** will sound. The system will remain active, and the buzzer will turn off once no motion is detected.

Extending the Project:

To make this security system more robust and advanced, consider adding the following features:

- **Camera Integration**: Use a camera module or connect the system to a **Raspberry Pi** to capture photos or video when motion is detected.

- **SMS or Email Alerts**: Use a **Wi-Fi module (ESP8266)** or **Ethernet shield** to send SMS or email alerts when motion is detected.

- **Multiple Sensors**: Integrate other sensors, such as door/window magnetic sensors, vibration sensors, or cameras, to enhance the security system.

- **Cloud Integration**: Store the captured data or event logs in the cloud for remote monitoring and analysis.

Conclusion

In this chapter, you learned how to create a **motion-activated security system** using **Arduino**, a **PIR motion sensor**, and a **buzzer**. We covered the basics of security systems and how sensors, cameras, and alarms are integrated into Arduino-based projects. This project demonstrates how Arduino can be used to monitor and secure an area by detecting motion and triggering alarms. With this knowledge, you can create more complex home security systems, integrating different sensors, cameras, and remote monitoring capabilities to protect your home or property. Keep exploring and enhancing your security systems!

CHAPTER 18

ARDUINO AND ARTIFICIAL INTELLIGENCE

In this chapter, we will explore how to integrate **Artificial Intelligence (AI)** into **Arduino projects**. While Arduino doesn't have the processing power of a typical AI system, it can still interact with AI models and perform simple AI tasks, such as basic machine learning models and object recognition. We will discuss how AI can be used in Arduino projects, how simple machine learning models can be implemented, and build a practical project—a **smart object recognition system**.

Basics of AI in the Context of Arduino

Artificial Intelligence (AI) refers to the simulation of human intelligence processes by machines. It involves algorithms and systems designed to mimic the way humans think, learn, and make decisions. In the context of Arduino, AI can be used to enhance projects by adding the ability to "learn" from data, make decisions, and even perform tasks like object recognition or speech recognition.

AI on Arduino:

Arduino doesn't have the processing power to run complex AI algorithms natively, but it can still be used to interact with AI models or perform basic AI tasks. For more computationally intensive AI tasks, Arduino can work with external processing units like **Raspberry Pi**, or **Edge AI** platforms.

Common AI Applications with Arduino:

- **Object recognition**: Using cameras and sensors to recognize and classify objects.
- **Voice recognition**: Using microphones and simple speech recognition models.
- **Motion detection**: Recognizing and tracking motion or gestures.
- **Decision-making systems**: Using data to make automated decisions.

Arduino typically interacts with AI models by sending sensor data to more powerful systems that process the data and then use the results to control actuators (e.g., motors, lights) or make decisions.

Simple Machine Learning Models with Arduino

Machine learning (ML) is a subset of AI that allows systems to learn from data and improve over time without explicit programming. On Arduino, you can use simple machine learning models that don't require extensive computational resources. Machine learning models for Arduino often focus on classification tasks or regression tasks, where the goal is to predict a category or value based on sensor data.

Training and Running Machine Learning Models:

While Arduino can't train large machine learning models due to its limited computational power, you can:

1. **Train the model externally**: Train a machine learning model on a more powerful system (e.g., a computer or a cloud service) and then deploy the model to Arduino for real-time predictions.

2. **Use pre-trained models**: Pre-trained models can be loaded onto the Arduino or an external device, and the

Arduino can feed data to the model and receive predictions.

Common Tools for Machine Learning with Arduino:

- **TensorFlow Lite for Microcontrollers**: A lightweight version of TensorFlow designed to run on embedded systems like Arduino.
- **Teachable Machine**: A simple tool from Google that allows you to train models for object recognition and upload them to Arduino-compatible devices.
- **Edge Impulse**: An embedded machine learning platform that can be used with Arduino to deploy machine learning models on microcontrollers.

Practical Project: Creating a Smart Object Recognition System

In this project, we will create a **smart object recognition system** using Arduino and a camera. The system will be able to recognize simple objects and take actions based on the objects it detects. While Arduino itself doesn't have enough processing power for advanced object recognition, we can use a simple external AI model to achieve this functionality.

Materials Needed:

- **Arduino board** (e.g., Arduino Uno or Arduino Nano 33 BLE Sense)
- **Camera module** (e.g., OV7670, or a camera module that works with Arduino)
- **AI model for object recognition** (can be trained using Teachable Machine or Edge Impulse)
- **MicroSD card module** (optional, for storing images or data)
- **Servo motor** or **LED** (to take action based on object recognition)
- **Jumper wires**
- **Breadboard** (optional)
- **Power supply** (for the camera and Arduino)

Step 1: Train an Object Recognition Model

We will use **Teachable Machine** to train an object recognition model. Teachable Machine allows you to create simple models for image recognition and then export them in a format compatible with microcontrollers like Arduino.

1. Go to Teachable Machine.
2. Choose the **Image Project** option.
3. Upload images of the objects you want the system to recognize (e.g., a cup, bottle, and book).

4. Train the model by clicking "Train Model."

5. After training, export the model for use with Arduino. You can export the model as a **TensorFlow Lite** model that can be used on microcontrollers.

Step 2: Upload the Model to Arduino

Once you have the model, use **TensorFlow Lite for Microcontrollers** to run the model on Arduino. You can use the **Arduino_TensorFlowLite** library to integrate the model into your Arduino code.

1. Install the **TensorFlow Lite for Microcontrollers** library via the Arduino Library Manager.

2. Use the exported model and upload it to your Arduino, along with the code that reads the camera data and makes predictions.

Step 3: Setting Up the Camera Module

You can use an **OV7670 camera module** or another compatible camera. The camera will send image data to Arduino, which will process the data using the trained AI model.

Wiring the Camera Module to Arduino:

- **OV7670 Camera Module** typically uses several pins for data transmission. Follow the datasheet to correctly connect it to the Arduino. For simplicity, you may choose a camera module that is compatible with the Arduino board you are using.

Step 4: Arduino Code for Object Recognition

Here's a simplified version of how the code might look, using **TensorFlow Lite** to run an object recognition model:

cpp

```cpp
#include <TensorFlowLite.h>
#include <SD.h>
#include <SPI.h>

const int cameraPin = 3; // Set the pin connected
to the camera
const int servoPin = 9;  // Pin connected to a
servo motor

// Load your TensorFlow Lite model here (this
would be a pre-trained model)
extern "C" {
  extern unsigned char model_data[];
}

// Create objects for running inference
```

```
tflite::MicroInterpreter* interpreter;
tflite::Model* model;

void setup() {
  Serial.begin(9600);

  // Initialize the SD card (if you want to store
images)
  if (!SD.begin()) {
    Serial.println("SD    card    initialization
failed!");
    return;
  }

  // Load the TensorFlow Lite model
  model = tflite::GetModel(model_data);
  interpreter                   =                new
tflite::MicroInterpreter(model,    tensor_arena,
kTensorArenaSize);

  // Initialize the camera and set up the servo
motor
  pinMode(servoPin, OUTPUT);
}

void loop() {
  // Capture image from the camera
  uint8_t* imageData = captureImageFromCamera();
```

```
// Process the image using the model
interpreter->SetInputTensor(imageData);
interpreter->Invoke();

// Read the result from the model and take
action
int recognizedObject = getRecognitionResult();

if (recognizedObject == 0) {  // For example,
0 could represent a "cup"
    Serial.println("Cup detected!");
    // Activate servo or LED
    digitalWrite(servoPin, HIGH);
  } else if (recognizedObject == 1) {  // 1 could
represent a "book"
    Serial.println("Book detected!");
    digitalWrite(servoPin, LOW);
  }

  delay(1000);
}


// Dummy function to represent capturing an image
from the camera
uint8_t* captureImageFromCamera() {
  // Replace with actual camera image capture
code
  static uint8_t dummyImage[128 * 128];
  return dummyImage;
```

```
}

// Dummy function to represent getting the
recognition result
int getRecognitionResult() {
  // Replace with actual object recognition code
  return random(0, 2);  // Randomly returns 0 or
1 for this example
}
```

Explanation:

- The **model_data** array contains the trained TensorFlow Lite model.
- The **captureImageFromCamera** function simulates capturing an image (you would replace this with actual image capture code).
- Based on the object recognition result, the system triggers the servo motor or takes other actions.

Conclusion

In this chapter, we learned how to incorporate **Artificial Intelligence (AI)** and **machine learning** into **Arduino projects**. We discussed how to create simple AI models using platforms like **Teachable Machine** and deploy them on Arduino for object recognition tasks. We built a **smart object recognition system** that uses a camera to identify objects and take action based on the recognition result. This chapter opens the door for more advanced AI and machine learning applications with Arduino, allowing you to build smarter devices and interactive systems. Keep experimenting with AI models to enhance your projects and explore new possibilities!

CHAPTER 19

POWERING YOUR ARDUINO PROJECTS

In this chapter, we'll explore how to properly power your **Arduino projects**. Understanding the power requirements for your Arduino is essential to ensure that it runs efficiently, especially in projects where portability or sustainability is important. We will look at the different **power sources** available, such as **batteries**, **USB**, and **solar power**, and provide a practical project on how to **power your Arduino projects with solar energy**.

Understanding Power Requirements for Arduino

Every electronic component, including the **Arduino** board itself, requires a specific amount of power to operate. The power requirements for an Arduino project depend on factors such as the board type, the sensors and actuators you're using, and the nature of your project (whether it needs to run on a portable battery or a continuous power supply).

Arduino Power Consumption:

- **Arduino Uno**: Typically requires 5V of power and consumes around 50mA of current during operation, but this can increase with the use of external components.
- **Arduino Nano**: Similar power requirements as the Uno but in a more compact form factor.
- **Arduino Mega**: Requires more power (around 70-100mA) due to the additional I/O pins and components.

In addition to the Arduino board itself, you need to consider the power consumption of external components, such as sensors, motors, and displays, which may require significantly more current.

Power Sources: Batteries, USB, and Solar

1. USB Power:

- **What it is**: Arduino boards can be powered directly through the **USB connection**. This is the most common and convenient power source for development and testing.
- **Voltage**: The USB port typically provides **5V**, which is the required voltage for most Arduino boards.

- **Limitations**: USB power is typically only suitable for development or testing in a stationary setup where the board is connected to a computer or USB power supply.

2. Batteries:

- **What they are**: Batteries provide a portable, mobile power source for Arduino projects. The most common types of batteries used are **AA batteries, Lithium-Ion** or **Lithium-Polymer (LiPo)** batteries, and **9V batteries**.
- **Voltage**: Most Arduino boards (like the Uno and Nano) can accept voltages from **6V to 12V** when supplied through the barrel jack or Vin pin.
- **Limitations**: The power output of the battery is limited, and the lifetime of your project depends on the type and capacity of the battery. Higher-power components like motors will drain the battery faster.

Common Battery Types:

- **AA Batteries**: Good for low-power projects.
- **Li-Ion/Li-Po Batteries**: Offer high energy density and are rechargeable, making them great for mobile projects.
- **9V Batteries**: Often used for portable Arduino projects, but not ideal for high-power applications.

3. Solar Power:

- **What it is**: **Solar panels** can be used to generate renewable energy to power your Arduino projects. Solar energy is ideal for outdoor or remote projects where other power sources may be unavailable or impractical.
- **Voltage and Current**: Solar panels come in various sizes and output voltages, so it's important to choose one that matches the power requirements of your Arduino and other components.
- **Limitations**: The power output of a solar panel can be affected by weather conditions, location, and time of day. It is also important to use a **solar charge controller** to manage the power distribution to ensure consistent operation.

Practical Project: Powering Your Arduino Projects with Solar Energy

In this project, we will demonstrate how to **power an Arduino project using solar energy**. This project will use a **solar panel**, a **solar charge controller**, and a **battery** to store energy and power an Arduino. We'll use a small solar panel to charge a battery, and the battery will then power the Arduino.

Materials Needed:

- Arduino board (e.g., Arduino Uno)
- **5V Solar Panel** (with enough current output for your project)
- **5V Solar Charge Controller** (e.g., TP4056 for Li-ion battery charging)
- **Lithium-Ion or LiPo Battery** (e.g., 18650 Li-ion battery)
- **Diode** (to prevent reverse current flow)
- **Jumper wires**
- **Breadboard** (optional)
- **Power Management Circuit** (optional, to regulate power output)

Wiring the Components:

1. **Solar Panel**: Connect the **positive** and **negative** terminals of the solar panel to the **solar charge controller** (using the input terminals marked as "+" and "-").
2. **Solar Charge Controller**:
   o Connect the **"B+"** and **"B-"** terminals of the charge controller to the battery terminals.
   o The charge controller will manage charging the battery and prevent overcharging.
3. **Battery**: Connect the battery to the charge controller.
4. **Arduino**: Use the **Vin** pin or **5V pin** on the Arduino to connect to the battery output of the charge controller. You

can use a **voltage regulator** if needed to ensure the voltage is stable.

5. **Diode**: Optionally, connect a **diode** in series with the battery to prevent current from flowing back to the panel when it is not generating power.

Code for Solar-Powered Arduino System:

cpp

```cpp
int sensorPin = A0;   // Sensor pin (for example,
a light sensor)
int sensorValue = 0; // Variable to store sensor
value

void setup() {
  Serial.begin(9600);        //   Start   serial
communication
}

void loop() {
  // Read the value from the sensor
  sensorValue = analogRead(sensorPin);

  // Print the sensor value to the serial monitor
  Serial.print("Sensor Value: ");
  Serial.println(sensorValue);
```

```
// Add additional code to perform actions based
on sensor value (e.g., turning on an LED or motor)
  delay(1000);    // Wait for a second before
reading again
}
```

Explanation:

- The **solar panel** will charge the **battery** during the day.
- The **solar charge controller** ensures the battery is charged properly and prevents damage from overcharging.
- The **Arduino** is powered by the battery, and it runs the code to read sensor values (e.g., a light sensor) or perform other tasks.
- This setup can be extended with sensors, motors, and other components that run on renewable energy.

Testing the Solar-Powered System:

1. **Connect the system**: Ensure the solar panel is receiving light and that the battery is charging through the solar charge controller.
2. **Test the Arduino**: Once the system is connected and powered, the Arduino will start running the code. You can

use a light sensor to test the data logging or add an actuator like an LED or motor to test the output.

3. **Monitor the Power**: Keep track of the battery level and ensure the solar panel is generating enough power to sustain the system. On sunny days, the panel should charge the battery effectively to power the Arduino.

Conclusion

In this chapter, you learned about the different **power sources** available for Arduino projects, including **USB**, **batteries**, and **solar power**. We discussed how to calculate power requirements and how to select appropriate power sources based on your project's needs. The **solar power project** demonstrated how to use a solar panel to charge a battery, which then powers the Arduino, providing an energy-efficient and sustainable solution for remote or outdoor projects.

Solar energy is an excellent option for powering Arduino projects that need to run independently, and with the growing interest in renewable energy, this chapter provides a foundation for further exploration into self-sustaining systems.

CHAPTER 20
TROUBLESHOOTING AND
DEBUGGING ARDUINO
PROJECTS

In this chapter, we will explore **troubleshooting and debugging techniques** for Arduino projects. Arduino projects, like any other electronic projects, may encounter issues that can be frustrating to diagnose. We'll cover some common issues you might face, how to resolve them, and how to use tools like the **Serial Monitor** for efficient debugging. Additionally, we'll discuss best practices for troubleshooting and ensure your projects run smoothly.

Common Issues with Arduino and How to Fix Them

When working with Arduino, you may run into various problems. Below are some of the most common issues and how to address them:

1. Arduino Not Powering On

- **Possible Causes**:
  - o **No power supply**: Ensure your Arduino is connected to a power source. If using USB, check if the USB cable is properly plugged in.
  - o **Incorrect voltage supply**: If using an external power source (e.g., battery or power adapter), make sure the voltage matches the Arduino's requirements (typically 5V for most Arduino boards).
- **Solution**: Check all connections and make sure your Arduino is receiving the correct power supply. If using a battery, make sure it has charge.

2. Uploading Code Fails

- **Possible Causes**:
  - o **Incorrect COM port**: The Arduino IDE may be trying to upload to the wrong port.
  - o **Wrong board selected**: Make sure the correct board is selected in the Arduino IDE under **Tools > Board**.
  - o **Driver issues**: Sometimes, the necessary drivers for your Arduino may not be installed correctly, especially for new boards or clones.
- **Solution**:
  - o Go to **Tools > Port** and make sure the correct COM port is selected.

- o Double-check that the correct board type is selected.
- o Reinstall or update the Arduino drivers if necessary.

3. No Response from Sensors or Components

- **Possible Causes**:
  - o **Wiring issues**: Double-check the connections between the Arduino and components.
  - o **Incorrect component initialization**: Sometimes libraries or code may fail to initialize sensors properly.
  - o **Power supply issues**: If the sensors or components require more power than what the Arduino can supply, this may cause malfunctions.
- **Solution**: Check the sensor wiring, ensure proper initialization in the code, and consider using an external power source for components that require more power.

4. Sensor Readings Are Incorrect

- **Possible Causes**:
  - o **Incorrect sensor calibration**: Some sensors need to be calibrated to provide accurate readings.

- o **Interference or noise**: External electrical noise can sometimes interfere with sensor readings.
- o **Faulty sensor**: The sensor itself might be defective.
- **Solution**:
  - o Review the sensor's datasheet and ensure it's correctly calibrated.
  - o Use **capacitors** or **shielding** to reduce noise.
  - o Test the sensor independently or replace it with a known working sensor to check for faults.

5. Components Not Responding to Code

- **Possible Causes**:
  - o **Syntax errors in the code**: Ensure your code is free of errors and functions properly.
  - o **Wrong pins or modes set**: Make sure the pins you're using are configured correctly (input vs. output).
  - o **Logical errors**: Sometimes, the code may contain logical errors, causing the wrong output.
- **Solution**: Check for errors in your code and verify pin configurations. Use the **Serial Monitor** to track variables and control flow.

Using the Serial Monitor for Debugging

The **Serial Monitor** is one of the most powerful debugging tools in the Arduino IDE. It allows you to print output from the Arduino to your computer's screen, providing insights into what's happening in your code. Here's how to effectively use it:

1. Printing Variables and Output:

You can use the `Serial.print()` or `Serial.println()` functions to display the values of variables, the state of the program, or debug messages. For example:

cpp

```
int sensorValue = 0;

void setup() {
  Serial.begin(9600);          //    Start    serial
communication at 9600 baud rate
}

void loop() {
  sensorValue = analogRead(A0);   // Read the
sensor value
  Serial.print("Sensor Value: ");
```

```
  Serial.println(sensorValue);      // Print the
sensor value to the Serial Monitor
  delay(1000);                      // Wait for 1
second
}
```

2. Debugging with Serial.print():

When your code isn't behaving as expected, use `Serial.print()` at various points to check if certain blocks of code are being reached or if variables are holding the expected values. For example:

cpp

```
int count = 0;

void loop() {
  Serial.print("Count: ");
  Serial.println(count);
  if (count == 5) {
    Serial.println("Count reached 5!");
  }
  count++;
  delay(1000);
}
```

This will show you the progression of the variable `count` and help you identify any logical errors.

3. Monitoring Program Flow:

Sometimes, the issue isn't with the values but with the flow of your program. Insert debug print statements at various places to see if the program is reaching certain functions or loops:

cpp

```cpp
void loop() {
  Serial.println("Start of loop");

  if (condition) {
    Serial.println("Condition met");
  }

  Serial.println("End of loop");
}
```

Best Practices for Efficient Troubleshooting

1. Break Down the Problem:

When you face an issue, break down the problem into smaller parts:

- Check if the **Arduino is working** independently (run a simple test, like the Blink example).
- **Test individual components** (sensors, actuators) separately.
- Debug the **wiring and connections** to ensure everything is correctly placed.

2. Use the Serial Monitor Liberally:

Use the **Serial Monitor** to display values of variables and track program flow. It's one of the most powerful tools for debugging, especially in the absence of a more advanced debugging tool. Print out key information to track the logic of your program.

3. Check Documentation and Resources:

When working with components or libraries, always refer to their datasheets, manuals, or online resources. Often, issues stem from incorrect wiring, misunderstandings of the component's behavior, or incorrect use of libraries.

4. Isolate and Replace:

If you suspect a particular component is faulty, try isolating it and testing it separately. If it doesn't work on its own, it's likely the problem. If it works separately, the issue may lie in how it's integrated with the rest of the system.

5. Start Simple:

If your complex project isn't working, simplify it. Start with a basic setup and gradually build it up. For example, if you're having trouble with a sensor, first test it by reading its data in isolation, then build up the complexity.

6. Use Online Communities:

If you're stuck, there's a large and active **Arduino community** online. Websites like **Arduino Stack Exchange**, **Instructables**, and the **Arduino forums** offer a wealth of knowledge from other users who may have faced similar issues.

Conclusion

In this chapter, we explored effective strategies for **troubleshooting and debugging Arduino projects**. We covered common issues that arise during development and the steps to resolve them, as well as how to use the **Serial**

Monitor to track variables and program flow for debugging purposes. By following best practices for troubleshooting, such as isolating the problem, checking connections, and using simple test cases, you can efficiently identify and fix issues in your Arduino projects. Debugging is a critical skill for any maker or engineer, and with the right techniques, you can keep your Arduino projects running smoothly.

CHAPTER 21

ADVANCED SENSORS AND MODULES

In this chapter, we will explore **advanced sensors** such as **gas sensors, pH sensors**, and **soil moisture sensors**, and learn how to integrate them into Arduino-based projects. These sensors are widely used for **environmental monitoring** applications, where data collection and analysis of natural conditions are crucial. We will discuss the working principles of these sensors, how to interface them with Arduino, and build a practical project—a **complete environmental monitoring system**.

Exploring Advanced Sensors: Gas, pH, and Soil Moisture Sensors

1. Gas Sensors

Gas sensors detect the presence and concentration of gases in the air, which is useful in a wide range of applications, such as air quality monitoring, safety systems, and industrial applications.

- **Types of Gas Sensors**:
  - ○ **MQ Series Sensors**: The **MQ** series of sensors (e.g., MQ-2, MQ-7, MQ-135) are commonly used to detect gases like **CO, CO2, NH3**, and **smoke**.
  - ○ **CCS811**: A sensor that measures **CO2** and **total volatile organic compounds (TVOCs)**, often used in indoor air quality monitoring.
- **How It Works**: Gas sensors typically have a sensitive material (like **semiconductor oxide** or **metal oxide**) that reacts when a gas is present. The resistance of the material changes, which is then measured by the Arduino to determine the gas concentration.

2. pH Sensors

pH sensors are used to measure the acidity or alkalinity of a solution. They are commonly used in **agriculture**, **aquariums**, and **water treatment** applications.

- **How It Works**: pH sensors work by detecting the hydrogen ion concentration in the liquid. The sensor typically generates a voltage proportional to the pH level, which the Arduino reads and converts to a pH value.

3. Soil Moisture Sensors

Soil moisture sensors are used to measure the water content of soil, making them essential in **agriculture** and **gardening**. These sensors help in determining the need for irrigation and maintaining optimal soil conditions.

- **How It Works**: Soil moisture sensors detect the dielectric constant of the soil, which changes with the water content. The sensor measures the resistance or capacitance between two electrodes to determine the moisture level.

Integrating Environmental Monitoring with Arduino

Arduino is well-suited for integrating these sensors into a single environmental monitoring system due to its low cost, ease of use, and large number of available libraries. By interfacing multiple sensors with an Arduino board, we can build systems to monitor **air quality**, **soil health**, and **water conditions**.

1. Interfacing Gas Sensors with Arduino

Gas sensors typically have **analog output** that corresponds to the concentration of gases. For instance, the **MQ-2** sensor has an analog pin that provides a voltage proportional to the amount of gas in the air.

- **Wiring the MQ-2** (as an example):
    - ○ Connect the **VCC** pin of the sensor to the **5V** pin on Arduino.
    - ○ Connect the **GND** pin of the sensor to **GND** on Arduino.
    - ○ Connect the **analog output** (A0) pin of the sensor to an **analog input pin** (e.g., **A0**) on the Arduino.

2. Interfacing pH Sensors with Arduino

pH sensors typically come with a **BNC** connector, and the output is usually in the form of an **analog voltage** that can be read by Arduino's analog pins.

- **Wiring the pH Sensor**:
    - ○ Connect the **VCC** pin of the sensor to **5V**.
    - ○ Connect the **GND** pin of the sensor to **GND** on Arduino.
    - ○ Connect the **analog output** pin of the pH sensor to an **analog input pin** (e.g., **A1**).

3. Interfacing Soil Moisture Sensors with Arduino

Soil moisture sensors usually have either **analog** or **digital output**. The **analog output** provides a variable voltage depending on the soil moisture level.

- **Wiring the Soil Moisture Sensor**:
    - Connect the **VCC** pin to **5V** on the Arduino.
    - Connect the **GND** pin to **GND**.
    - If using an **analog sensor**, connect the **analog output** to an analog pin (e.g., **A2**).

Practical Project: Building an Environmental Monitoring System

In this project, we'll combine the **gas sensor, pH sensor, and soil moisture sensor** into a single **environmental monitoring system**. The system will monitor the air quality, soil moisture, and pH levels, and display the data on a simple **LCD screen**.

Materials Needed:

- Arduino board (e.g., Arduino Uno)
- **MQ-2 Gas Sensor** (for air quality)
- **pH Sensor** (for measuring pH levels in water)
- **Soil Moisture Sensor** (for measuring soil moisture)

- **LCD Display** (e.g., 16x2 LCD)
- Jumper wires
- Breadboard (optional)
- **Power supply** (for Arduino)

Wiring the Components:

1. **MQ-2 Gas Sensor**:
   - Connect the **VCC** pin to **5V**.
   - Connect the **GND** pin to **GND**.
   - Connect the **analog output** to **A0** on Arduino.

2. **pH Sensor**:
   - Connect the **VCC** pin to **5V**.
   - Connect the **GND** pin to **GND**.
   - Connect the **analog output** to **A1** on Arduino.

3. **Soil Moisture Sensor**:
   - Connect the **VCC** pin to **5V**.
   - Connect the **GND** pin to **GND**.
   - Connect the **analog output** to **A2** on Arduino.

4. **LCD Display**:
   - Connect the **VCC** and **GND** pins of the LCD to **5V** and **GND** on Arduino.
   - Connect the **SDA** and **SCL** pins of the LCD to the corresponding **A4** (SDA) and **A5** (SCL) pins on the Arduino Uno.

Arduino Code for Environmental Monitoring System:

cpp

```cpp
#include <LiquidCrystal_I2C.h>

// Pin assignments
int gasPin = A0;      // MQ-2 gas sensor pin
int pHPin = A1;       // pH sensor pin
int moisturePin = A2; // Soil moisture sensor pin

LiquidCrystal_I2C lcd(0x27, 16, 2); // LCD setup
(I2C address, columns, rows)

void setup() {
  Serial.begin(9600);     //     Start     serial
communication
  lcd.begin();          // Initialize the LCD
  lcd.print("Environmental Monitor");
  delay(2000);
}

void loop() {
  // Read sensor values
  int gasValue = analogRead(gasPin);     // Read
gas sensor value
  int pHValue = analogRead(pHPin);       // Read
pH sensor value
```

215

```
  int moistureValue = analogRead(moisturePin);
// Read moisture sensor value

  // Display data on LCD
  lcd.clear();
  lcd.setCursor(0, 0);
  lcd.print("Gas: ");
  lcd.print(gasValue);                          //
Display gas value
  lcd.setCursor(0, 1);
  lcd.print("Moist: ");
  lcd.print(moistureValue);                     //
Display soil moisture value

  // Send data to Serial Monitor
  Serial.print("Gas Value: ");
  Serial.println(gasValue);
  Serial.print("Soil Moisture: ");
  Serial.println(moistureValue);
  Serial.print("pH Value: ");
  Serial.println(pHValue);

  delay(1000); // Delay before taking the next
readings
}
```

Explanation:

- The **MQ-2 sensor** reads the gas levels in the air, and its output is displayed on the LCD.
- The **soil moisture sensor** measures the moisture level in the soil and is shown on the LCD.
- The **pH sensor** reads the pH level of the water and prints it to the **serial monitor**.
- The **LCD** shows the real-time values of the gas and soil moisture levels.

Testing the Environmental Monitoring System

1. **Upload the code** to your Arduino and open the **Serial Monitor** to see the output.
2. **Observe the LCD screen**: The values of gas, soil moisture, and pH levels should be displayed on the screen.
3. **Change the environmental conditions** (e.g., add water to the soil or expose the gas sensor to smoke) and see how the system reacts to changes in the environment.

Conclusion

In this chapter, we explored **advanced sensors** like gas, pH, and soil moisture sensors and learned how to integrate them into an **environmental monitoring system**. We built a practical system that monitors the air quality, soil moisture, and pH levels using Arduino. With these sensors, you can create powerful systems for monitoring natural conditions in agriculture, environmental monitoring, or even smart home applications. By expanding on this project, you can incorporate other sensors and create more complex environmental monitoring solutions.

CHAPTER 22

INTERFACING ARDUINO WITH OTHER PLATFORMS

In this chapter, we will explore how to interface **Arduino** with other platforms, such as **Raspberry Pi** and **cloud services** like **Google Firebase**. By combining Arduino with other microcontrollers and cloud platforms, we can build more powerful and flexible systems that can be controlled remotely, analyzed in real-time, or integrated with other devices. We will also build a practical project that demonstrates **cross-platform communication** using Arduino.

Connecting Arduino with Raspberry Pi and Other Microcontrollers

Arduino can communicate with other microcontrollers or platforms like **Raspberry Pi**, **ESP32**, or **ESP8266** to enhance functionality and add more capabilities to your projects. Let's explore two common approaches for connecting Arduino with these platforms.

1. Connecting Arduino with Raspberry Pi

The **Raspberry Pi** is a powerful single-board computer that can run a full operating system (such as **Raspbian**) and has more computing power compared to Arduino. When combined with Arduino, it can handle complex tasks such as data processing, image recognition, or running web servers, while Arduino can handle real-time sensor data collection and control tasks.

Methods for Connecting Arduino to Raspberry Pi:

1. **USB Serial Connection**: The easiest way to connect Arduino and Raspberry Pi is through a USB cable. Arduino is connected to the Raspberry Pi as a serial device, allowing the Pi to send commands or receive data from the Arduino.

   o **How It Works**: The Raspberry Pi sends commands via **serial communication** over USB, and the Arduino responds to these commands.

2. **GPIO Pins**: You can use **General Purpose Input/Output (GPIO)** pins on the Raspberry Pi to

connect to the Arduino's pins for direct communication.

- o **How It Works**: You can communicate via **I2C**, **SPI**, or **serial communication** over the GPIO pins, depending on your project's needs.

Wiring and Example of Serial Communication:

1. Connect Arduino to the Raspberry Pi via **USB**.
2. On the Raspberry Pi, you can communicate with Arduino using Python or the **Serial Monitor** on the Raspberry Pi.

Example in Python (on Raspberry Pi) to communicate with Arduino via **USB**:

```python
python

import serial
import time

# Set up the serial connection
ser = serial.Serial('/dev/ttyUSB0', 9600)   # Adjust port based on your setup

# Send data to Arduino
ser.write(b'Hello Arduino')

# Wait for a response
```

```
time.sleep(1)

# Read data from Arduino
response = ser.readline()
print(response.decode('utf-8'))

ser.close()
```

2. Connecting Arduino with Other Microcontrollers (e.g., ESP32, ESP8266)

Microcontrollers like the **ESP32** or **ESP8266** are equipped with **Wi-Fi capabilities**, allowing for wireless communication between devices.

Methods for Connecting Arduino to Other Microcontrollers:

1. **Wi-Fi Communication**: You can use **Wi-Fi modules** (like ESP8266 or ESP32) to enable communication between Arduino and other devices over the internet.
2. **Serial Communication (UART)**: Similar to how you connect Arduino with Raspberry Pi, you can use serial communication to send data between Arduino and these microcontrollers.

Example: **Arduino (with ESP8266) sending data to another ESP32 over Wi-Fi**.

Using Arduino with Cloud Services like Google Firebase

Arduino can be connected to **cloud services** like **Google Firebase**, a real-time database, for storing and retrieving data remotely. Firebase offers an easy-to-use solution for cloud-based storage and can be used to log sensor data, control devices, or monitor systems remotely.

Steps for Connecting Arduino to Google Firebase:

1. **Create a Firebase Project**:
   - Go to Firebase and create a new project.
   - Enable **Realtime Database** and configure it.

2. **Install Firebase Libraries**:
   - Install the **Firebase Arduino library** in the Arduino IDE. This will allow Arduino to interact with the Firebase API.

3. **Configure Firebase with Arduino**:
   - Use the **Wi-Fi module (ESP8266/ESP32)** to connect Arduino to the internet.
   - Use Firebase's **REST API** to read and write data to your Firebase database.

Wiring:

For this project, you will need an **ESP8266** or **ESP32** to connect to the internet. Arduino will send data to Firebase via HTTP requests.

Example Code for Sending Data to Firebase (using ESP8266):

cpp

```cpp
#include <ESP8266WiFi.h>
#include <FirebaseArduino.h>

// Replace with your network credentials
const char* ssid = "your_network";
const char* password = "your_password";

// Replace with your Firebase project credentials
#define                         FIREBASE_HOST
"your_project_id.firebaseio.com"
#define FIREBASE_AUTH "your_firebase_auth_token"

void setup() {
  Serial.begin(115200);

  // Connect to Wi-Fi
  WiFi.begin(ssid, password);
  while (WiFi.status() != WL_CONNECTED) {
    delay(1000);
```

```
    Serial.println("Connecting to WiFi...");
  }
  Serial.println("Connected to WiFi");

  // Connect to Firebase
  Firebase.begin(FIREBASE_HOST, FIREBASE_AUTH);

  // Write some data to Firebase
  Firebase.setInt("sensor/temperature", 25);  //
Sending temperature data
  if (Firebase.failed()) {
    Serial.print("Setting/Updating        data
failed:");
    Serial.println(Firebase.error());
  }
}

void loop() {
  // You can add code to read sensors and upload
data periodically
}
```

Explanation:

- This code connects the **ESP8266** to Wi-Fi, then connects
  to **Firebase** and sends a value (e.g., temperature data) to
  a   specific   location   in   the   database
  (sensor/temperature).

Practical Project: Creating a Cross-Platform Communication System

In this practical project, we will create a **cross-platform communication system** that allows Arduino to communicate with both **Raspberry Pi** and **Google Firebase**. We will build a system where data from Arduino sensors (such as temperature or humidity) will be sent to both a **Raspberry Pi** (for local processing) and **Firebase** (for remote cloud storage and monitoring).

Materials Needed:

- **Arduino board** (e.g., Arduino Uno or Nano)
- **ESP8266 or ESP32** (for Wi-Fi communication)
- **Raspberry Pi** (with Python installed)
- **Temperature/Humidity Sensor** (e.g., DHT11/DHT22)
- **Firebase Account**
- **Jumper wires**
- **Breadboard** (optional)

Project Overview:

1. **Arduino Side**: The Arduino will collect sensor data and send it over Wi-Fi to both the Raspberry Pi and Firebase.

2. **Raspberry Pi Side**: The Raspberry Pi will receive the data from the Arduino and store or process it locally.

3. **Firebase**: The Arduino will also send the data to Firebase for remote storage and monitoring.

Steps:

1. **Setup Firebase**:
   o Follow the steps mentioned earlier to set up Firebase and create a project.

2. **Arduino Code**:
   o The Arduino will read data from a temperature sensor (like DHT22) and send it to both the Raspberry Pi (over USB or serial communication) and Firebase (over Wi-Fi using ESP8266 or ESP32).

3. **Raspberry Pi Python Script**:
   o The Raspberry Pi will receive the data via **serial communication** and store it in a local file or process it.

4. **Firebase**:
   o The Arduino will send the sensor data to Firebase using the **REST API** and store it in a **Realtime Database**.

Conclusion

In this chapter, we explored how to interface **Arduino** with other platforms like **Raspberry Pi** and **cloud services** like **Google Firebase**. We learned how to connect Arduino to **Raspberry Pi** using serial or GPIO pins for communication, how to send data from Arduino to the cloud using Firebase, and how to create a **cross-platform communication system**. These skills allow you to create more complex and scalable projects, where data can be monitored and controlled both locally and remotely. By connecting multiple platforms and using cloud services, you can extend the capabilities of your Arduino projects to build integrated systems for home automation, environmental monitoring, and more.

CHAPTER 23

POWER MANAGEMENT IN ARDUINO PROJECTS

In this chapter, we will explore **power management** techniques to make your **Arduino projects** more efficient in terms of energy consumption. Power efficiency is crucial for projects that run on **battery power** or are designed to operate in remote locations where power supply is limited. We will discuss using **low-power Arduino boards**, how to take advantage of **sleep modes**, and provide a practical project on creating a **battery-powered Arduino project** with low energy consumption.

Introduction to Power Efficiency in Electronics

Power efficiency refers to the ability of an electronic device or system to perform its intended functions using the least amount of electrical power possible. Power management is especially important in projects that require long operation times without access to a continuous power supply, such as:

- **Battery-powered projects**: Devices like weather stations, wearable sensors, and remote monitors.
- **Portable applications**: Drones, robots, or any device that needs to operate in the field.
- **Energy-harvesting systems**: Projects that rely on solar power or other renewable sources.

Efficient use of power extends the **battery life** of your projects, reduces maintenance costs, and makes your projects more sustainable. Arduino offers several techniques to improve power efficiency in your projects.

Using Low-Power Arduino Boards and Sleep Modes

1. Low-Power Arduino Boards

Certain **Arduino boards** are designed with **low-power consumption** in mind. For example:

- **Arduino Pro Mini**: It operates at a lower current draw (compared to an Arduino Uno) and is ideal for battery-powered applications.
- **Arduino Nano 33 BLE**: A low-power version of the Arduino Nano, using a **Bluetooth Low Energy (BLE)** connection for wireless communication.

- **Arduino MKR Series**: These boards are optimized for low-power applications and come with integrated communication modules (e.g., Wi-Fi, LoRa, or GSM) that are also designed to be energy-efficient.

When choosing a low-power Arduino board, consider the following:

- The **current draw** of the board at different operating states.
- The availability of power-saving modes, such as sleep and deep sleep.
- The **voltage requirements** and whether the board can be powered by a lower-voltage source (e.g., a 3.7V LiPo battery).

2. Arduino Sleep Modes

Sleep modes are one of the most effective ways to reduce the power consumption of an Arduino project when the device is idle or not actively processing data. By putting the microcontroller to sleep, you can drastically reduce its current draw.

Arduino offers several **sleep modes** through the **LowPower** library. Here's a brief overview of common sleep modes:

- **Idle Mode**: The CPU is stopped, but the system clock continues to run. This mode uses less power than normal operation but allows you to keep the timers running.

- **Standby Mode**: The CPU and system clock are stopped, but the **watchdog timer** and **external interrupts** still function. This is a low-power mode suitable for situations where the Arduino must wake up in response to an external event.

- **Power-down Mode**: The CPU, system clock, and peripherals are all stopped. Only the **interrupts** and **watchdog timer** are active. This is the most power-efficient mode.

By using these sleep modes, your Arduino can operate for **longer periods** on a single battery charge.

Practical Project: Creating a Battery-Powered Project with Low Energy Consumption

Let's create a **battery-powered environmental monitoring system** using **Arduino**. In this project, we will use a **DHT11 temperature and humidity sensor** and a **light sensor** to monitor the environmental conditions. The Arduino will only wake up periodically to take readings, then go back to sleep, consuming minimal power.

Materials Needed:

- **Arduino Pro Mini** (or another low-power Arduino board)
- **DHT11 Temperature and Humidity Sensor**
- **Light Sensor** (e.g., LDR or photoresistor)
- **3.7V LiPo Battery** (or any suitable rechargeable battery)
- **Voltage Regulator** (to step down to 5V if necessary)
- **Power Management Circuit** (optional, to monitor battery voltage)
- **Breadboard and jumper wires**
- **OLED Display** (optional, to display sensor readings)

Wiring the Components:

1. **DHT11 Sensor**:
   - Connect the **VCC** pin of the DHT11 sensor to **5V** (or **3.3V** depending on your Arduino board).
   - Connect the **GND** pin to **GND**.
   - Connect the **DATA** pin to **digital pin 2** on Arduino.

2. **Light Sensor (LDR)**:
   - Connect one end of the **LDR** to **5V** and the other end to **analog pin A0** on Arduino. Use a **10k ohm resistor** between the LDR and **GND** for a voltage divider.

3. **LiPo Battery**:

 o Connect the **positive** terminal of the battery to the **RAW** pin on the Arduino Pro Mini.

 o Connect the **negative** terminal of the battery to **GND**.

Arduino Code for Low-Power Environmental Monitoring System:

cpp

```cpp
#include <DHT.h>
#include <LowPower.h>

#define DHTPIN 2            // Pin connected to
the DHT11 sensor
#define DHTTYPE DHT11       // DHT11 sensor type

DHT dht(DHTPIN, DHTTYPE);

void setup() {
  // Start serial communication
  Serial.begin(9600);
  dht.begin();              // Initialize DHT sensor
}

void loop() {
  // Read temperature and humidity
```

```
float humidity = dht.readHumidity();
float temperature = dht.readTemperature();

// Check if the readings are successful
if (isnan(humidity) || isnan(temperature)) {
  Serial.println("Failed to read from DHT
sensor!");
  } else {
  Serial.print("Temperature: ");
  Serial.print(temperature);
  Serial.print("°C  Humidity: ");
  Serial.print(humidity);
  Serial.println("%");
  }

// Read light sensor (LDR)
int lightLevel = analogRead(A0);
Serial.print("Light Level: ");
Serial.println(lightLevel);

// Sleep for 8 seconds before the next reading
LowPower.powerDown(SLEEP_8S,          ADC_OFF,
BOD_OFF);
}
```

Explanation:

- **DHT11 Sensor**: Reads temperature and humidity data. If the sensor fails to read the data, it prints an error message.

235

- **Light Sensor**: Reads the light level from an LDR (Light Dependent Resistor) and prints it to the Serial Monitor.
- **LowPower Library**: The Arduino goes into **power-down mode** for 8 seconds after taking readings, reducing power consumption significantly. The **ADC** (Analog-to-Digital Converter) and **BOD** (Brown-Out Detection) are turned off during sleep to save energy.

Testing the System:

1. **Upload the code** to your Arduino board.
2. **Monitor the Serial Monitor** to check the sensor readings.
3. After 8 seconds, the Arduino will go into sleep mode and wake up to take another reading. The readings should be printed periodically, with the Arduino remaining in low-power mode between readings.

Power Consumption:

- When the Arduino is active, it consumes around **30-50mA** (depending on the sensors and the board).
- In sleep mode, the current consumption drops significantly to around **5-10mA**.
- With this setup, the system will run for an extended period on a **3.7V LiPo battery**.

Conclusion

In this chapter, we explored **power management** techniques for Arduino projects, focusing on how to create **low-power systems** using **sleep modes** and **low-power Arduino boards**. By utilizing power-saving techniques, such as putting the Arduino to sleep between tasks, we can create efficient, battery-powered systems that can operate for extended periods. The **environmental monitoring project** demonstrates how to collect sensor data while minimizing power consumption, making it ideal for remote or portable applications. By applying these techniques, you can design energy-efficient projects that can run on minimal power, ensuring longer battery life and reducing the need for frequent recharges or replacements.

CHAPTER 24

CUSTOMIZING ARDUINO SHIELDS AND PCBS

In this chapter, we will explore the process of **customizing Arduino shields and designing custom PCBs (Printed Circuit Boards)**. Custom shields and PCBs allow you to create Arduino-compatible hardware tailored specifically to your project needs. By designing and fabricating your own hardware, you can enhance your projects with specialized functions, more robust connectivity, and better integration. We will go over the basics of creating shields and PCBs, and we will complete a practical project where we design a custom **Arduino shield**.

Basics of Creating Custom Shields and PCBs

1. Understanding Arduino Shields

An **Arduino shield** is a **modular board** that can be plugged directly into the Arduino's pins to add specific functionality. Shields are designed to easily stack on top of an Arduino, making them convenient for adding sensors, communication modules, or output devices like motors and displays.

Customizing Arduino Shields

- **What is a Custom Shield?**: A **custom shield** is a tailored board designed to sit on top of an Arduino and provide additional features specific to your project. For example, you might create a shield that interfaces with a motor driver, adds extra sensor inputs, or provides custom displays.

- **Common Uses for Custom Shields**:
  - o **Motor drivers** for controlling DC motors, stepper motors, or servos.
  - o **Sensor interfaces** for adding specialized sensors like temperature, humidity, or gas sensors.
  - o **Communication shields** for adding Wi-Fi, Bluetooth, or LoRa communication capabilities.

- **How to Design a Custom Shield**:
  - o **Pinout Considerations**: Ensure the pins of your shield align correctly with the Arduino's headers. If your shield adds new pins or features, ensure they don't conflict with existing pins used by the Arduino.
  - o **Power Distribution**: You'll need to account for **power** requirements, especially if your shield

will be powering motors, sensors, or other power-hungry components.

- o **Shield Size and Mounting**: Custom shields must fit within the standard **Arduino footprint**. Be sure to leave space for connectors, components, and headers.

2. Understanding Printed Circuit Boards (PCBs)

A **PCB** is a physical platform that connects electronic components through copper traces, which provide electrical paths between them. Creating a custom PCB is a more advanced approach than using shields but offers more flexibility and integration options.

Steps to Design a Custom PCB:

1. **Schematic Design**: The first step in creating a custom PCB is to design a schematic, which is a diagram that shows how all the components are connected.

2. **PCB Layout**: Once the schematic is complete, you'll lay out the components and route the electrical connections on the board. This step involves placing components in a way that ensures minimal interference and optimizes space.

3. **Fabrication**: After designing the PCB, you can send the files to a PCB manufacturer to produce your board. These

manufacturers typically offer options for **single-layer** or **multi-layer** boards.

- **Tools for Designing PCBs**:
    - o **KiCad**: Free and open-source PCB design software.
    - o **Eagle**: A popular PCB design tool, which offers both free and paid versions.
    - o **Altium Designer**: A high-end, professional PCB design tool used in industry.

Practical Project: Designing a Custom Arduino Shield

In this project, we will design a simple **custom Arduino shield** that adds **two buttons** and **two LEDs**. This shield will allow us to control two LEDs through button presses, with each button corresponding to an LED.

Materials Needed:

- **Arduino board** (e.g., Arduino Uno)
- **Breadboard and jumper wires**
- **LEDs** (x2)
- **Push buttons** (x2)
- **Resistors** (220Ω for LEDs, 10kΩ for buttons)

- **PCB Design Software** (e.g., KiCad or Eagle)
- **Arduino-compatible headers**

Step 1: Design the Circuit

Let's start by designing the circuit that we'll be implementing on the custom shield.

1. **Buttons**:
   - Each button will be connected to a **digital input pin** on the Arduino. One leg of each button is connected to **GND**, and the other leg goes to the input pin (e.g., **pins 2 and 3**).
   - A **pull-down resistor** (10kΩ) is used to ensure the input pin reads LOW when the button is not pressed.
2. **LEDs**:
   - Each LED will be connected to **digital output pins** on the Arduino (e.g., **pins 4 and 5**).
   - A **220Ω resistor** is used in series with each LED to limit the current.

Step 2: Schematic Design

You can use **KiCad** or **Eagle** to draw the schematic of this circuit. The schematic will show how the buttons, LEDs, and Arduino pins are connected.

- **Arduino Pins**: Assign **pins 2 and 3** for the buttons and **pins 4 and 5** for the LEDs.
- **Button to Ground**: Connect one side of each button to **GND**, and the other to the corresponding pin.
- **LEDs with Resistors**: Connect the anodes (positive legs) of the LEDs to **pins 4 and 5** and the cathodes (negative legs) to **GND** through 220Ω resistors.

Step 3: PCB Layout

Once the schematic is complete, you can move on to designing the **PCB layout**:

1. **Component Placement**: Position the components on the PCB. Ensure that the buttons and LEDs are arranged in a user-friendly way and the headers for connecting the shield to the Arduino are placed correctly.
2. **Routing**: Connect the components with copper traces, ensuring that the signals follow the correct paths. Avoid crossovers and ensure adequate space between traces.
3. **Final Check**: Ensure that the PCB dimensions match the Arduino board's shield footprint (68.6mm x 53.4mm).

Step 4: Fabrication

Once the design is ready, export the **Gerber files** (which are the standard file format used for PCB manufacturing) from your PCB design software. Send these files to a **PCB manufacturer** (e.g., JLCPCB or PCBWay) to fabricate your custom shield.

You can also **order a set of headers** for easy mounting of your shield onto the Arduino.

Step 5: Soldering and Assembly

After receiving the fabricated PCB:

1. **Solder the Components**: Use a soldering iron to attach the components (buttons, LEDs, resistors, and headers) to the PCB.
2. **Test the Shield**: Insert the shield into the Arduino, upload the code, and check if the buttons control the LEDs as expected.

Arduino Code for Custom Shield

cpp

```
const int buttonPin1 = 2;   // Button 1 pin
const int buttonPin2 = 3;   // Button 2 pin
```

244

```
const int ledPin1 = 4;      // LED 1 pin
const int ledPin2 = 5;      // LED 2 pin

void setup() {
  pinMode(buttonPin1, INPUT);  // Set button pins
as input
  pinMode(buttonPin2, INPUT);
  pinMode(ledPin1, OUTPUT);    // Set LED pins as
output
  pinMode(ledPin2, OUTPUT);
}

void loop() {
  // Read button states
  int buttonState1 = digitalRead(buttonPin1);
  int buttonState2 = digitalRead(buttonPin2);

  // Control LEDs based on button press
  if (buttonState1 == HIGH) {
    digitalWrite(ledPin1, HIGH);  // Turn on LED
1
  } else {
    digitalWrite(ledPin1, LOW);   // Turn off LED
1
  }

  if (buttonState2 == HIGH) {
    digitalWrite(ledPin2, HIGH);  // Turn on LED
2
```

```
} else {
    digitalWrite(ledPin2, LOW);    // Turn off LED
2
    }
}
```

Explanation:

- The code reads the button inputs and turns the corresponding LEDs on or off based on whether the buttons are pressed.

Conclusion

In this chapter, we explored how to **customize Arduino shields** and **design custom PCBs** for your projects. We discussed the process of designing a custom Arduino shield, from creating the schematic to fabricating and assembling the PCB. With this knowledge, you can create Arduino-compatible hardware tailored to your needs, enhancing your projects with additional features or more integrated solutions. The **custom Arduino shield project** provided a practical example of how to design, build, and use custom hardware to expand the functionality of your Arduino projects.

CHAPTER 25

ARDUINO FOR WEARABLE TECHNOLOGY

In this chapter, we will explore how **Arduino** can be used in the world of **wearable technology**. Wearable devices have become increasingly popular in recent years, with applications ranging from fitness trackers to smartwatches. Arduino provides a great platform to experiment with and build your own wearable technology, thanks to its flexibility and large ecosystem of sensors. We'll cover how to use Arduino for wearable projects, such as **fitness trackers** and **smartwatches**, and we'll build a **step counter** as a practical project.

Introduction to Wearable Devices

Wearable technology refers to electronic devices designed to be worn on the body, typically incorporated into clothing, accessories, or even directly on the skin. Wearables have evolved from simple devices like pedometers to complex gadgets that can track health metrics, monitor activity levels, and interact with other smart devices. Some common examples include:

- **Fitness trackers**: Devices that monitor steps, heart rate, calories burned, and more.
- **Smartwatches**: Wrist-worn devices that integrate with smartphones to display notifications, monitor health, and provide various apps.
- **Health monitoring devices**: Wearables that track specific health metrics like sleep patterns, blood pressure, or glucose levels.

Key Features of Wearable Devices:

1. **Sensors**: Wearables typically rely on sensors to collect data. Common sensors include **accelerometers**, **gyroscopes**, **heart rate monitors**, and **GPS modules**.
2. **Low Power Consumption**: Wearable devices need to be energy-efficient to ensure they can operate for extended periods, often using **battery-powered** systems.
3. **Comfort and Design**: Wearables need to be lightweight and compact to ensure comfort during prolonged use.
4. **Wireless Communication**: Wearables often communicate wirelessly using **Bluetooth** or **Wi-Fi** to connect with smartphones or other devices for data synchronization and control.

Using Arduino for Fitness Trackers and Smartwatches

1. Arduino in Wearables

Arduino is an excellent platform for creating wearable projects because of its flexibility, accessibility, and the variety of components and modules available. You can easily add sensors to an Arduino board, gather data, and display it on small screens or transmit it wirelessly.

Components for Wearable Projects:

- **Accelerometer**: Measures the movement and orientation of the device, which is crucial for activity tracking.
- **Gyroscope**: Measures rotational movements, complementing the accelerometer for full 3D motion tracking.
- **Heart Rate Sensor**: A sensor like the **Pulse Sensor** can track your heart rate and send it to the Arduino for monitoring.
- **OLED Display**: A small, low-power display to show information like step count, time, or heart rate.
- **Bluetooth Module (HC-05 or HC-06)**: For wirelessly communicating with smartphones or other Bluetooth-enabled devices.

- **Battery**: A rechargeable battery (like a **Li-Po battery**) to power your wearable device.

2. Designing Wearable Devices with Arduino

- **Compact Design**: Wearable devices need to be compact and lightweight, so choosing a small Arduino board, such as the **Arduino Nano** or **Arduino Pro Mini**, is ideal.
- **Low Power Consumption**: Use Arduino's **sleep modes** to conserve power when the device is not in use.
- **Wireless Communication**: Adding Bluetooth allows you to sync data with a mobile device or display notifications directly on the wearable.

Practical Project: Building a Simple Step Counter

In this project, we will build a **simple step counter** using **Arduino** and an **accelerometer** (such as the **ADXL345**). The project will measure movement and detect steps, providing basic functionality for a fitness tracker.

Materials Needed:

- **Arduino Nano** (or any small Arduino board)

- **ADXL345 Accelerometer** (or any similar 3-axis accelerometer)
- **OLED Display** (128x64, for displaying step count)
- **Push button** (to reset the step count)
- **Battery** (e.g., 3.7V LiPo battery for portable power)
- **Jumper wires** and **breadboard**

Wiring the Components:

1. **ADXL345 Accelerometer**:
   - **VCC** to **5V** on Arduino.
   - **GND** to **GND** on Arduino.
   - **SDA** to **A4** on Arduino (for I2C communication).
   - **SCL** to **A5** on Arduino (for I2C communication).

2. **OLED Display**:
   - **VCC** to **5V** on Arduino.
   - **GND** to **GND** on Arduino.
   - **SDA** to **A4** (I2C).
   - **SCL** to **A5** (I2C).

3. **Push Button**:
   - One leg of the button to **GND**.
   - The other leg to **D2** (for step count reset).

Arduino Code for Step Counter:

cpp

```
#include <Wire.h>
#include <Adafruit_Sensor.h>
#include <Adafruit_ADXL345_U.h>
#include <Wire.h>
#include <Adafruit_GFX.h>
#include <Adafruit_SSD1306.h>

#define SCREEN_WIDTH 128
#define SCREEN_HEIGHT 64
#define OLED_RESET -1
Adafruit_SSD1306          display(SCREEN_WIDTH,
SCREEN_HEIGHT, &Wire, OLED_RESET);

// Create an instance of the accelerometer
Adafruit_ADXL345_Unified      accel         =
Adafruit_ADXL345_Unified(12345);

// Step count variables
int stepCount = 0;
int threshold = 15; // Set a movement threshold
for detecting steps
long lastStepTime = 0;

const int buttonPin = 2;  // Pin for the reset
button

void setup() {
  // Initialize serial communication
  Serial.begin(9600);
```

```
  // Initialize the OLED display
  if         (!display.begin(SSD1306_I2C_ADDRESS,
OLED_RESET)) {
    Serial.println(F("SSD1306        allocation
failed"));
    for (;;);
  }
  display.display();
  delay(2000);
  display.clearDisplay();

  // Initialize the accelerometer
  if (!accel.begin()) {
    Serial.println("Couldn't       find       the
accelerometer");
    for (;;);
  }

  // Set the range of the accelerometer
  accel.setRange(ADXL345_RANGE_2G);

  // Set the button pin as input
  pinMode(buttonPin, INPUT_PULLUP);
}

void loop() {
  // Read accelerometer data
  sensors_event_t event;
```

```
accel.getEvent(&event);

// Calculate the movement magnitude
long  movement  =  abs(event.acceleration.x)  +
abs(event.acceleration.y)                      +
abs(event.acceleration.z);

// If  movement  exceeds  threshold  and  enough
time has passed, count a step
if   (movement  >   threshold  &&  millis()  -
lastStepTime > 200) {
    stepCount++;
    lastStepTime = millis();  // Update the time
of the last step
  }

// Check if the reset button is pressed
if (digitalRead(buttonPin) == LOW) {
    stepCount = 0;   // Reset step count
    delay(500);      // Debounce the button
  }

// Display the step count on the OLED
display.clearDisplay();
display.setTextSize(1);
display.setTextColor(SSD1306_WHITE);
display.setCursor(0,0);
display.print("Steps: ");
display.println(stepCount);
```

```
display.display();
delay(100);
}
```

Explanation:

- **Accelerometer**: The **ADXL345** accelerometer measures movement in three axes (X, Y, and Z). We use the combined acceleration values to detect steps.
- **Threshold**: When the total movement exceeds a certain threshold, a step is counted. The value of `threshold` can be adjusted based on how sensitive you want the step detection to be.
- **OLED Display**: The step count is displayed on the **OLED display** in real-time.
- **Button Reset**: A **push button** is used to reset the step count.

Testing the Step Counter:

1. **Upload the code** to your Arduino and connect the components as described.
2. **Observe the OLED display**: The step count will increase each time you make a movement that exceeds the threshold.
3. **Test the reset function**: Press the reset button to set the step count back to zero.

Power Considerations for Wearables

Wearable devices need to be energy-efficient, especially if they are battery-powered. In the step counter example, we can make the device more power-efficient by implementing **sleep modes** in the Arduino, similar to what we discussed in previous chapters. Using **low-power Arduino boards** and **power-saving techniques** (e.g., deep sleep modes between measurements) can drastically extend battery life.

Conclusion

In this chapter, we explored how to create **wearable devices** with **Arduino**, focusing on fitness trackers and smartwatches. We designed a **step counter** as a practical project, using an **accelerometer** to track movement and display the step count on an **OLED display**. Wearables can be made even more effective with **low-power designs**, ensuring long battery life, which is crucial for wearable applications. With the knowledge gained in this chapter, you can start building more advanced wearable devices, such as smartwatches, health trackers, and personal fitness monitors.

CHAPTER 26

BRINGING IT ALL TOGETHER: FINAL PROJECT

In this final chapter, we will **combine** all the skills we've learned throughout the book to create a **comprehensive project** that integrates multiple components. Our final project will be a **Smart Home Automation System** using **Arduino**, where we will control various aspects of a smart home, such as lights, temperature, and security, all from a centralized system.

This project will combine concepts such as **sensor integration**, **motor control**, **cloud communication**, **power management**, and **user interface design**. Let's explore how to create a **fully functional smart home automation system** using Arduino.

Combining Skills Learned in the Previous Chapters

Over the course of the book, we have covered a wide range of topics. Here's a quick recap of the key concepts we'll use in this final project:

- **Sensors and Actuators**: We've worked with various sensors such as **temperature sensors, motion sensors**, and **light sensors**. For actuators, we've used components like **motors, LEDs**, and **relays**.

- **Wireless Communication**: We've explored ways to wirelessly communicate between devices using **Wi-Fi, Bluetooth**, and **cloud services** like **Google Firebase**.

- **Power Management**: We've discussed how to reduce power consumption and extend battery life, which is crucial for battery-powered projects like wearables and remote systems.

- **Custom Shields and PCBs**: While not necessary for the final project, the concepts of customizing shields and designing your own PCBs can be applied if needed for expanding the system.

- **Arduino Programming and Debugging**: We've learned how to write code to interact with sensors, control actuators, and debug issues using the **Serial Monitor**.

Creating a Comprehensive Project that Integrates Multiple Components

The goal of this project is to create a **smart home automation system** where:

1. **Sensors**: Monitor environmental conditions (temperature, motion, light).
2. **Actuators**: Control devices like lights and fans based on sensor data.
3. **Wireless Communication**: Use **Wi-Fi** to send data to the cloud for remote monitoring and control.
4. **User Interface**: Provide a simple **web interface** or mobile app to control the system remotely.

System Overview:

- **Temperature and Humidity**: Use a **DHT11** or **DHT22** sensor to monitor room temperature and humidity.
- **Motion Detection**: Use a **PIR motion sensor** to detect movement in rooms and automatically turn on lights.
- **Light Control**: Control lights using **relays** connected to Arduino.
- **Cloud Integration**: Send temperature, humidity, and motion data to **Google Firebase** for remote monitoring.
- **Power Management**: Use **sleep modes** to reduce power consumption when the system is idle.

Final Project: Building a Smart Home Automation System Using Arduino

Materials Needed:

- **Arduino Uno** (or any Arduino-compatible board)
- **DHT11** or **DHT22** sensor (for temperature and humidity)
- **PIR Motion Sensor** (for motion detection)
- **Relay Module** (to control lights/fans)
- **LEDs** (optional, for testing light control)
- **Wi-Fi Module (ESP8266 or ESP32)** for cloud connectivity
- **Power Supply** (e.g., 5V USB adapter or battery pack)
- **Jumper Wires** and **Breadboard**
- **Google Firebase Account** for cloud communication
- **Smartphone or computer** to control the system remotely

Step 1: Wiring the Components

1. **DHT11 Temperature and Humidity Sensor**:
   - Connect the **VCC** pin to **5V**.
   - Connect the **GND** pin to **GND**.
   - Connect the **DATA** pin to **digital pin 2** on the Arduino.

2. **PIR Motion Sensor**:
   - Connect the **VCC** pin to **5V**.
   - Connect the **GND** pin to **GND**.

o Connect the **OUTPUT** pin to **digital pin 3** on the Arduino.

3. **Relay Module**:

   o Connect the **VCC** pin to **5V**.

   o Connect the **GND** pin to **GND**.

   o Connect the **IN1** pin of the relay module to **digital pin 4** on Arduino (this controls the relay).

   o Use the relay to control an appliance (e.g., a fan or light) by connecting the relay to its power source.

4. **Wi-Fi Module (ESP8266 or ESP32)**:

   o For **ESP8266**, connect the **TX/RX** pins to **RX/TX** on Arduino (ensure proper voltage levels).

   o If using **ESP32**, the process is similar but requires a different pinout. Ensure you have the correct libraries installed.

Step 2: Setting Up Google Firebase

1. **Create a Firebase project**:

   o Go to Google Firebase, create a new project, and enable the **Realtime Database**.

   o Get the **Firebase URL** and **Authentication token** that will be used in your Arduino code.

2. **Firebase Data Structure**:

○ Your Firebase Realtime Database will store data from sensors. For example:

```json
json

{
  "temperature": 24.5,
  "humidity": 65,
  "motion": "detected"
}
```

Step 3: Arduino Code for Smart Home Automation System

```cpp
cpp

#include <Wire.h>
#include <ESP8266WiFi.h>
#include <FirebaseArduino.h>
#include <DHT.h>

// Replace with your network credentials and
Firebase details
const char* ssid = "your_ssid";
const char* password = "your_password";
#define                         FIREBASE_HOST
"your_firebase_project.firebaseio.com"
#define FIREBASE_AUTH "your_firebase_auth_token"
```

```
// Define the DHT sensor and relay pin
#define DHTPIN 2
#define RELAY_PIN 4
DHT dht(DHTPIN, DHT22);

const int motionSensorPin = 3;

void setup() {
  Serial.begin(9600);
  WiFi.begin(ssid, password);

  while (WiFi.status() != WL_CONNECTED) {
    delay(1000);
    Serial.println("Connecting to WiFi...");
  }

  Serial.println("Connected to WiFi");

  Firebase.begin(FIREBASE_HOST, FIREBASE_AUTH);
  dht.begin();
  pinMode(RELAY_PIN, OUTPUT);
  pinMode(motionSensorPin, INPUT);
}

void loop() {
  // Read temperature and humidity
  float temperature = dht.readTemperature();
  float humidity = dht.readHumidity();
```

```
// Read motion sensor
int            motionState            =
digitalRead(motionSensorPin);

// Send data to Firebase
Firebase.setFloat("temperature", temperature);
Firebase.setFloat("humidity", humidity);
Firebase.setInt("motion", motionState);

// Control relay based on motion
if (motionState == HIGH) {
  digitalWrite(RELAY_PIN, HIGH);  // Turn on
light/fan
  } else {
  digitalWrite(RELAY_PIN, LOW);   // Turn off
light/fan
  }

  delay(5000); // Delay for 5 seconds before next
reading
}
```

Explanation:

- **Wi-Fi**: The system connects to your home Wi-Fi network.
- **Firebase**: The temperature, humidity, and motion sensor data are sent to Firebase in real-time.

- **Relay Control**: The relay is controlled based on the motion sensor data, turning on or off connected devices (lights, fans).

- **Cloud Monitoring**: You can view and control this data from your Firebase console or integrate it into a mobile app for real-time updates.

Step 4: Testing the System

1. **Upload the code** to your Arduino or ESP8266/ESP32 board.

2. **Monitor Firebase**: Check the Firebase database for the live temperature, humidity, and motion data.

3. **Control the Relay**: When motion is detected, the relay should turn on the connected device (e.g., a light or fan). When no motion is detected, the device will turn off.

4. **Cloud Monitoring**: You can access the Firebase Realtime Database from your phone or computer to monitor sensor data remotely.

Conclusion

In this chapter, we brought everything together by creating a **smart home automation system** using Arduino. This project integrated multiple components, such as **sensors** (temperature, humidity, motion), **actuators** (relays for controlling lights or fans), **cloud communication** (Firebase for remote monitoring), and **wireless communication** (Wi-Fi for cloud connectivity). This project serves as an excellent example of how Arduino can be used in real-world applications, integrating sensors, actuators, and cloud platforms to create a connected system. With this knowledge, you can expand and customize your own smart home systems, adding more features and improving functionality.

www.ingramcontent.com/pod-product-compliance
Lightning Source LLC
Chambersburg PA
CBHW070940050326
40689CB00014B/3275